Student Workbook

From School to Work

Teacher's Annotated Workbook

J.J. Littrell, Ed. D.
Arizona State University
Tempe, Arizona

Annie Hunter Clasen
Instructor
Aparicio-Levy Technical Center
Tampa, Florida

Peggy Pearson
Diversified Career Technology Coordinator
Simmons Career Center
Plant City, Florida

Publisher
The Goodheart-Willcox Company, Inc.
Tinley Park, Illinois
www.g-w.com

Introduction

This *Student Workbook* is designed for use with the *From School to Work* text. As you complete the activities in this *Workbook*, you review the facts and concepts presented in the text. The overall objective of these activities is to help you make a smooth transition from your classroom to a meaningful job in the workplace.

The activities in this *Workbook* are divided into chapters corresponding to the chapters in the text. By reading the text first, you have the information needed to complete the activities. Try to complete each without referring to the text. Then check the text for answers to questions you could not complete. Compare your answers with the information in the text.

The activities will help you gain the skills you need to succeed in the workplace. Some activities, such as crossword puzzles, true/false questions, and math exercises, have "right" answers. Other activities ask you to evaluate various situations, make comparisons, or draw your own conclusions. These activities have neither "right" nor "wrong" answers since they are designed to stimulate creative thinking and help you develop ideas. Do your best to give thoughtful consideration to all your responses.

ISBN 978-1-59070-938-2

1 2 3 4 5 6 7 8 9 – 09 – 14 13 12 11 10 09 08

Teacher's Annotated Workbook

ISBN 978-1-59070-939-9

1 2 3 4 5 6 7 8 9 – 09 – 14 13 12 11 10 09 08

Contents

Part 3 Career Planning

Part 4   The Job Hunt

Part 5   Job Satisfaction

Making the Transition from School to Work

Getting to Know Your Classmates

Activity A

Chapter 1

Name_____

Date_____**Period**_____

Interview someone in your class. Find the answers to the following questions and ask two questions of your own. Use the information to prepare an introduction that mentions five interesting facts about the person.

Name of classmate: (Student response.)_____

1. At what grade level are you? (Student response.)_____

2. How long have you been a student at this school? (Student response.)_____

3. What other schools have you attended? (Student response.)_____

   _____

4. Why did you choose to take this class? (Student response.)_____

   _____

5. Are you presently employed?_____ If so, where? (Student response.)_____

   _____

   A. How long have you worked there? (Student response.)_____

   B. What other employment or volunteer work have you done? (Student response.)_____

   _____

   C. How did you obtain your employment or volunteer work? (Student response.)_____

   _____

6. Do you have any hobbies or sports interests? (Student response.)_____

   _____

7. What do you do in your spare time? (Student response.)_____

8. What extracurricular activities were you involved in last year? Explain why you *were* or *were not* involved. (Student response.)_____

   _____

9. What extracurricular activities do you plan to pursue this school year? (Student response.)_____

   _____

10. What was your favorite movie in the past year? (Student response.)_____

    _____

(Continued)

Name_____

11. What was the most meaningful event for you this past year? (Student response.) _____

_____

12. What was the most embarrassing thing that ever happened to you? (Student response.) _____

_____

_____

13. What do you plan to do after graduation? (Student response.) _____

_____

14. What are your parents' or guardians' occupations? Briefly describe their jobs. (Student response.) ___

_____

_____

15. List three adjectives to describe yourself:

    A. (Student response.) _____

    B. (Student response.) _____

    C. (Student response.) _____

16. Finish the following sentence: "If I had my choice, I'd take a job in (Student response.) _____

    because_____ .

17. Who has influenced you most and in what ways? (Student response.) _____

_____

18. Which two places would you like to visit? (Student response.) _____

_____

_____

19. Write two additional questions here and your responses.

    Question: (Student response.) _____

    Response: (Student response.) _____

    _____

    _____

    Question: (Student response.) _____

    Response: (Student response.) _____

    _____

    _____

Candidates for Work-Based Education

Activity B

Chapter 1

Name _____

Date _____ Period _____

Read two case studies about students who are candidates for work-based learning programs in their schools. From the information given in the text, explain how each student could benefit from a work-based learning program. Be prepared to discuss your responses in class.

Case 1. John wants to own his own landscape business someday. During his senior year, he can participate in a school-to-work experience in turf management at a local golf course. He is not sure the experience will help him. John asks your advice. What would you tell him?

(Sample response.) John should participate in the school-to-work experience. The program will allow him to gain

experience. It will also help him decide if he is sure about his career choice.

_____

_____

_____

_____

_____

_____

_____

_____

_____

_____

Case 2. Susan will be a senior this fall. After graduation she plans to go to college. She says she wants to major in veterinary medicine, but her best grades are not in science. If she could only get some experience at an animal clinic, she would be more certain of whether all the hard work required to become a veterinarian will result in a job she loves. Also, she needs a job now to earn money for college. How could a work-based learning program benefit Susan?

(Sample response.) Susan can get related experience and decide if a veterinarian career is right for her. She can

also save the money she earns for college.

_____

_____

_____

_____

_____

_____

_____

_____

_____

The School-to-Work Experience

Activity C

Chapter 1

Name_____

Date_____Period_____

Read the statements below and write the missing terms in the crossword puzzle.

```
                    1
                    S
                    P
          2                     3
          W O R K B A S E D
                    N           U           4
                    S           P           P
      5             O     6       7
      S             R     I     M E N T O R
      T             R     N       R       G
      A                   T       V       R
      T                   E       I       A
      I                   R       S       M
  8
  C O O R D I N A T O T
  N                       S       R
                          H
                          I
                  9
                  C O O P E R A T I V E
```

Across

2. School programs that prepare students for the workplace are called _____-_____ learning programs.

7. The coworker who will help you learn your new job is called the work-based _____.

8. The special teacher or counselor at school who assists students in a work-based learning program is known as the school-to-work _____.

9. A school program that alternates students between a paid job experience at a work site and time in the classroom is called _____ education.

Down

1. A work-based mentor is also called a training _____.

3. The _____ is your boss in the workplace.

4. The school-to-work coordinator is sometimes called the _____ coordinator.

5. The training _____ is the job site where a student works to learn job skills.

6. A program that offers paid or unpaid work experience to learn about a job or industry is an _____.

The Benefits of School-to-Work Programs

Activity D

Chapter 1

Name_____

Date _____ Period _____

Ken graduated from East High School in June. The week after graduation, he was employed in a full-time job that offered an opportunity for advancement. He wrote the letter below to his former school-to-work coordinator. Read Ken's letter and answer the questions that follow.

612 W. Maple Drive
Newland, AZ 85011
June 20, 20XX

Dear Mr. Hudson:

    It's only one week after graduation, and I have some good news to share with you. I already have a job as a technician at the Edison Electronic Company! It's a great job, and I even have a chance to be promoted if I get more training and do well on the job.

    Actually, the reason I'm writing is to let you know that your Industrial Cooperative Education class helped me get the job. Your class meant a great deal to me. It gave me a chance to work in industrial electronics during my senior year.

    I remember you told us that most adults spend much of their lives working. That made me realize a person's work should be a good experience. For that reason, I wanted to get some work experience before graduating from high school. I also wanted to find out if I would like electronics work. By participating in the school-to-work program, I found that I enjoyed the work very much. The work experience gave me a chance to apply some of the skills I learned in your electronics classes. By listening and learning on the job, I also gained new skills. Of course, earning a paycheck was nice, too!

    That school-to-work experience was important for another reason—it gave me the feeling of being an important part of the workforce. I felt I was treated not just as a student, but also as an adult with a job that mattered. At the work site, I also learned to work with my supervisors and other employees.

    I know my on-the-job experience in high school persuaded my current employer to hire me over other job applicants. I also know that my school-to-work experience will help me advance in the future.

Thank you for helping me.

Sincerely,

Ken McDaniel

Ken McDaniel

1. Why did Ken write to Mr. Hudson? to tell him about his new job and how the work-based learning program benefited him _____

_____

_____

(Continued)

Name_____

2. What high school subject did Mr. Hudson teach Ken? <u>industrial cooperative education</u>

3. For what reason did Ken want to participate in the school-to-work program? <u>to get work experience</u> <u>while in school and to find out if he would enjoy working in electronics</u>

4. Did Ken earn money during his school-to-work experience? <u>yes</u>

5. Why did Ken feel adultlike in his school-to-work program? <u>because he was treated as a worker, not a</u> <u>student</u>

6. List five benefits Ken received from his on-the-job experience. <u>(List five:) gained work experience before</u> <u>graduating from high school, learned that he enjoyed working in electronics, learned to work with super-</u> <u>visors and other employees, earned a paycheck, gained the job experience to obtain a full-time job, learned</u> <u>skills that were useful in the new job</u>

7. Imagine you are Ken's current employer. Write a letter to Mr. Hudson explaining why you hired a high school graduate with work-based learning experience. <u>(Student response.)</u>

What Are Your Workplace Skills?

Activity E   Name _____

Chapter 1   Date _____ Period _____

Review the knowledge and skills in the chart and rate your workplace readiness by checking the appropriate box for each. Then answer the questions that follow. (Chart answers are student response.)

Workplace Skills	Very Good	Good	Fair	Poor	Do Not Possess
Academic Foundations					
Read and comprehend written material.					
Compose neat and accurately written messages.					
Calculate a percentage discount on an item.					
Apply basic measurement methods.					
Correctly demonstrate common lab or workshop procedures.					
Communications					
Make oral presentations well.					
Write an effective letter.					
Listen to instructions to complete a new task.					
Use nonverbal communication well.					
Summarize complex facts into charts and diagrams.					
Problem Solving and Critical Thinking					
Prioritize work assignments.					
Apply established procedures to new projects.					
Identify problems and form possible answers.					
Compare and evaluate alternative solutions.					
Form new, creative approaches to challenges.					
Information Technology Applications					
Use a computer to create various documents and diagrams.					
Research and collect data from reliable Internet sources.					
Organize, maintain, and transfer computer files correctly.					
Use presentation software for effective communications.					
Use spreadsheet and database applications correctly.					
Systems					
Explain and draw an organizational chart.					
Diagram the steps of a problem's possible solutions.					
Monitor, correct, and improve your work performance.					
Break down a complex task into component parts.					
Understand roles within teams and work units.					
Safety, Health, and Environment					
Know and follow all safety rules.					
Wear personal protective equipment.					
Identify common safety hazards and emergency procedures they require.					
Identify personal behaviors that are unsafe.					
Educate others to health and safety awareness.					
Leadership and Teamwork					
Contribute to positive group efforts.					
Teach others new work skills.					
Eliminate barriers in work relationships.					
Negotiate to gain an agreement.					
Work well with others from different cultures.					

(Continued)

Name_____

Workplace Skills	Very Good	Good	Fair	Poor	Do Not Possess
Ethics and Legal Responsibilities					
Distinguish between ethical and unethical conduct at work.					
Explain plagiarism.					
Identify when permission is needed before certain information is used.					
Name the laws that regulate your workplace.					
Identify situations that may pose legal problems.					
Employability and Career Development					
Develop a career plan.					
Know and understand the value of transferable skills.					
Explain the qualifications needed before entering the career of your choice.					
Identify the importance of workplace dress and appearance standards.					
Explain what you must do to get a promotion.					
Technical Skills					
Judge the best procedures, tools, or machines to use.					
Examine new technology's impact on your work.					
Operate equipment according to guidelines.					
Identify reasons for wrong results from tools or machines.					
Follow maintenance procedures to prevent failures.					

How can you improve the *Fair* or *Poor* skills you identified?

(Student response.)

_____

_____

_____

_____

How can you acquire the skills you do *not* possess?

(Student response.)

_____

_____

_____

_____

How will your skills influence your career choice?

(Student response.)

_____

_____

_____

_____

_____

Understanding Work-Based Learning

Training Agreement Responsibilities

Activity A

Chapter 2

Name_____

Date_____Period_____

After reviewing a copy of the work-based learning training agreement used by your school, summarize in your own words the responsibilities required of each person who signs the agreement.

1. Employer's responsibilities: (Student response.)

_____

_____

_____

_____

_____

_____

_____

_____

_____

_____

_____

_____

_____

_____

A. Which responsibility do you think is the most important? Why? (Student response.)

_____

_____

_____

B. How important are the other responsibilities the employer has after signing the agreement? _____

(Student response.)

_____

_____

(Continued)

Name_____

2. Your responsibilities: (Student response.) _____

_____

_____

_____

_____

_____

_____

_____

A. Which responsibility do you think is most important? Why? (Student response.) _____

_____

_____

B. How important are the other responsibilities you have after signing the agreement? _____

(Student response.) _____

_____

3. Program coordinator's responsibilities: (Student response.) _____

_____

_____

_____

4. Parent's or guardian's responsibilities: (Student response.) _____

_____

_____

_____

5. What is the purpose of the training agreement? to assure the employer that the student is committed to

the work experience; to assure the student that the employer is committed to training him or her to do the

job; to assure the parent(s) or guardian that the student is involved in a well-planned educational experi-

ence; to assure the school-to-work coordinator that all parties understand their responsibilities and are

committed to the student having a successful work experience _____

_____

_____

_____

Getting a Social Security Card

Activity B

Chapter 2

Name _____

Date _____ Period _____

Complete the application for a social security card by filling in every item that applies to you.
(Answers are student response.)

SOCIAL SECURITY ADMINISTRATION
Application for a Social Security Card

Form Approved
OMB No. 0960-0066

1	**NAME** TO BE SHOWN ON CARD	First	Full Middle Name	Last
	FULL NAME AT BIRTH IF OTHER THAN ABOVE	First	Full Middle Name	Last
	OTHER NAMES USED			

2 MAILING ADDRESS Do Not Abbreviate
Street Address, Apt. No., PO Box, Rural Route No.
City | State | ZIP Code

3 CITIZENSHIP (Check One)
☐ U.S. Citizen ☐ Legal Alien Allowed To Work ☐ Legal Alien **Not** Allowed To Work (See Instructions On Page 2) ☐ Other (See Instructions On Page 2)

4 SEX ☐ Male ☐ Female

5 RACE/ETHNIC DESCRIPTION (Check One Only - Voluntary)
☐ Asian, Asian-American or Pacific Islander ☐ Hispanic ☐ Black (Not Hispanic) ☐ North American Indian or Alaskan Native ☐ White (Not Hispanic)

6 DATE OF BIRTH Month, Day, Year

7 PLACE OF BIRTH (Do Not Abbreviate) City State or Foreign Country FCI Office Use Only

8 A. MOTHER'S NAME AT HER BIRTH First Full Middle Name Last Name At Her Birth
B. MOTHER'S SOCIAL SECURITY NUMBER (See instructions for 8B on Page 2)

9 A. FATHER'S NAME First Full Middle Name Last
B. FATHER'S SOCIAL SECURITY NUMBER (See instructions for 9B on Page 2)

10 Has the applicant or anyone acting on his/her behalf ever filed for or received a Social Security number card before?
☐ Yes (If "yes", answer questions 11-13.) ☐ No (If "no," go on to question 14.) ☐ Don't Know (If "don't know," go on to question 14.)

11 Enter the Social Security number previously assigned to the person listed in item 1.

12 Enter the name shown on the most recent Social Security card issued for the person listed in item 1.
First Middle Name Last

13 Enter any different date of birth if used on an earlier application for a card. Month, Day, Year

14 TODAY'S DATE Month, Day, Year

15 DAYTIME PHONE NUMBER ( ) – Area Code Number

I declare under penalty of perjury that I have examined all the information on this form, and on any accompanying statements or forms, and it is true and correct to the best of my knowledge.

16 YOUR SIGNATURE

17 YOUR RELATIONSHIP TO THE PERSON IN ITEM 1 IS:
☐ Self ☐ Natural Or Adoptive Parent ☐ Legal Guardian ☐ Other (Specify)

DO NOT WRITE BELOW THIS LINE (FOR SSA USE ONLY)

NPN			DOC	NTI	CAN		ITV
PBC	EVI	EVA	EVC	PRA	NWR	DNR	UNIT

EVIDENCE SUBMITTED

SIGNATURE AND TITLE OF EMPLOYEE(S) REVIEWING EVIDENCE AND/OR CONDUCTING INTERVIEW

DATE

DCL   DATE

The Training Plan

Activity C   Name_____

Chapter 2   Date_____Period_____

Complete the training plan cover page below. Use O*NET™, The Occupational Information Network (www.online.onetcenter.org) to locate your job title, number, and description. Then compare the job description given on O*NET with your present job responsibilities. Based on this comparison, prepare a short job description for your present job.   (Answers are student response.)

Training Plan for Work-Based Learning

Student's Name _____

Social Security No._____ Home Phone_____

Student's Career Objective_____

Employer _____

Employer's Address _____

Dates of Employment _____

Supervisor _____

Job Title and Number (O*NET) _____

Job Description_____

_____

_____

_____

_____

_____

_____

_____

We agree that the tasks, duties, and/or competencies identified here will be included in the training plan for the student's training while enrolled in the Work-Based Learning Program.

Employer _____ Date_____

Program Coordinator_____ Date_____

Student_____ Date_____

Know the Law

Activity D	Name_____
Chapter 2	Date_____ Period_____

Read the following cases. Then answer the questions below and provide explanations.

Case 1. Wayne has been employed as a trainee in a print shop for one month and receives less than minimum wage for his work. According to the FLSA, have Wayne's rights been violated? _no, because_

employers may pay employees less during a training period

Case 2. Karen and Don work for an insurance company. They were hired at the same time and do the same jobs. One day, Don found out that Karen was paid more for her work. Have Don's rights been violated?

yes, because the Equal Pay Act requires equal pay to employees of both sexes for doing equal jobs

What should Don do? _file a complaint with the U.S. Dept. of Labor or Equal Employment Opportunity Commission_

Case 3. Linda works as a telephone operator for $9.00 an hour. One week she worked 48 hours. According to the FLSA, is Linda entitled to overtime pay? _yes, $468_

Assuming overtime is paid at a rate of 1½ times the regular rate for each hour worked beyond 40, what is Linda's pay for the week?

Case 4. Jamilla and Bill work in a large department store doing the same job with the same responsibilities. Jamilla has worked there for one year, while Bill has worked there for nine years. Jamilla found out Bill is paid a wage higher than hers. Were Jamilla's rights violated? _no, because pay exceptions may_

occur for differences in seniority

Case 5. Wu has been employed at a card shop for three years. She works 40 hours per week, receiving less than minimum wage for her work. According to the FLSA, have Wu's rights been violated? _yes,_

because minimum wage is the lowest hourly pay rate that most employees must receive and Wu's job does not

qualify for an exemption

What should she do? _file a complaint with the Wage and Hour Division of the U.S. Department of Labor_

Case 6. Sherry is 16 years old and works in the office of a large meatpacking plant. She would prefer to operate a meat-cutting machine, but the plant supervisor refuses to give her the job. According to the FLSA, have Sherry's rights been violated? _no, because she is too young to lawfully operate a_

meat-cutting machine, which is considered a hazardous job

Case 7. Hasem is a server in a restaurant. He is paid $5.50 per hour. According to the FLSA, have Hasem's rights been violated? _no, because food service workers earn tips so they may lawfully be paid less_

than minimum wage

Case 8. Montel is 16 years old and in a job training program to become a customer service representative. He makes $5.00 per hour. According to the FLSA, have Montel's rights been violated? _no, employees_

may be paid less during a training period

Case 9. Renalia is 18 years old. She works in a supermarket deli. She uses a meat and cheese slicer every day. According to the FLSA, have Renalia's rights been violated? _no, this is not considered a_

hazardous occupation for people 18 and older

Your Study Habits

Activity E	**Name** _____	
Chapter 2	**Date** _____ **Period** _____	

Think about your study habits. Respond to the statements below, then analyze your responses. (There are no right or wrong answers.)   (Answers are student response.)

Yes	No	Sometimes	
_____	_____	_____	1. When it's time to study, I cannot seem to get started.
_____	_____	_____	2. I find it easy to keep my mind on what I am studying.
_____	_____	_____	3. I reread a line two or three times to get the meaning.
_____	_____	_____	4. I do not understand the words that I read.
_____	_____	_____	5. I like to read.
_____	_____	_____	6. I do not remember what I read.
_____	_____	_____	7. I do not take very good notes.
_____	_____	_____	8. I like to write.
_____	_____	_____	9. I usually do not know the assignment.
_____	_____	_____	10. I do not want to ask for help.
_____	_____	_____	11. I study with music playing.
_____	_____	_____	12. I like to participate in class.
_____	_____	_____	13. I use class time to socialize with my friends.
_____	_____	_____	14. When taking notes in class, I write down every word the teacher says.
_____	_____	_____	15. When taking notes in class, I write down the most important points to help me remember the main ideas and facts.
_____	_____	_____	16. I keep a separate notebook for each class.
_____	_____	_____	17. I usually do the easiest assignments first.
_____	_____	_____	18. I complete class assignments every day.
_____	_____	_____	19. I make a list of tasks I must complete each day.
_____	_____	_____	20. I put the most important tasks to be done first on my list.

Explain what your answers to these statements reveal about your study habits.

_____

_____

_____

What steps could you take to improve your study habits?

_____

_____

_____

Organizing Your Schedule

Activity F

Chapter 2

Name_____

Date_____ Period_____

As a work-based learning student, you will probably need to adjust your schedule in order to meet the required hours at school and at work. Use the chart below to keep track of how you spend your weekday time. Chart the time you spend at school, at work, studying, sleeping, and doing other activities throughout the day. Then analyze the finished chart and answer the following questions. (Be prepared to discuss how this activity helped you.)   (Schedule is student response.)

Time	Monday	Tuesday	Wednesday	Thursday	Friday

(Continued)

Name_____

1. How many hours during the week did you spend   (Student response.)

   in class? _____   sleeping? _____

   at work? _____   commuting? _____

   studying? _____   other? _____

2. What are your time wasters? _(Student response.)_____

   _____

   _____

3. If you could eliminate (or reduce) one time waster from the chart, which one would it be? Explain. _____

   _(Student response.)_____

   _____

4. How much uninterrupted time do you have for

   important tasks? _(Student response.)_____

   yourself? _(Student response.)_____

5. Do you have any free time to spend as you please? Explain. _(Student response.)_____

   _____

6. Are you allowing yourself enough time to study? Explain. _(Student response.)_____

   _____

7. Are you getting enough rest? Explain. _(Student response.)_____

   _____

8. For which important activity can you never seem to find enough time? _(Student response.)____

   _____

9. How might you be able to make time for important activities? _(Student response.)_____

   _____

   _____

   _____

10. What does *organizing your schedule in order of priority* mean? _giving the most time to the most important_

    tasks; placing the most important tasks in your schedule first, then organizing the rest of your time around them

11. How can an organized schedule give you more free time? _(Sample response.) If you schedule your_

    highest-priority tasks at appropriate times and follow the schedule, you will waste less time and have more

    blocks of time for free time.

12. What changes, if any, would you make in your weekday schedule? _(Student response.)_____

    _____

    _____

What Your Employer Expects

An Employer's View

Activity A

Chapter 3

Name _____

Date _____ Period _____

Interview an employer to obtain answers to the following questions and directions. Discuss the interview in class.

1. What do you expect of an employee? _(Student response.)_ _____

_____

2. How important is it for an employee to have good attendance on the job? _(Student response.)_ _____

_____

3. List at least three good qualities an employee should have. _(Student response.)_ _____

_____

_____

4. List at least three bad habits an employee should avoid. _(Student response.)_ _____

_____

_____

5. In what ways does attitude affect an employee's job performance? _(Student response.)_ _____

_____

6. Define _employee loyalty._ _(Student response.)_ _____

_____

7. How are employees expected to dress while on the job? _(Student response.)_ _____

_____

8. How can having courteous employees in the workplace benefit your business? _(Student response.)_

_____

9. What should an employee do after finishing an assigned job? _(Student response.)_ _____

_____

10. For what reasons would you fire an employee? _(Student response.)_ _____

_____

11. Describe the perfect employee. _(Student response.)_ _____

_____

12. How important is teamwork at your workplace? _(Student response.)_ _____

_____

_____

Personal Qualities on the Job

Activity B

Chapter 3

Name_____

Date_____Period_____

Imagine you are an employer. Which of the following employee work traits would be most important to you and your business? Work with a group to rank the following employee traits in order of importance, with *1* most important and *15* least important. Then report your group's top five choices to the class.
(Rankings are student response.)

_____ confidentiality

_____ cooperation

_____ courtesy

_____ excellent job performance

_____ good attendance

_____ good health and fitness

_____ honesty

_____ initiative

_____ loyalty

_____ neat personal appearance

_____ organizational skills

_____ positive attitude

_____ punctuality

_____ receptive to constructive criticism

_____ strong work ethic

_____ teamwork skills

What other personal qualities might an employer desire in an employee that are not listed above?_____

(Answers may vary.) cheerfulness, determination, persistence

_____

_____

_____

_____

_____

_____

_____

_____

Personal Traits

Activity C   Name _____

Chapter 3   Date _____ Period _____

Complete the puzzle by writing the correct personal traits in the spaces. Use the definitions below for clues.

1   R E S **P** O N S I B L E
2   A P P **E** A R A N C E
3 C O O P E **R** A T I O N
4   H O N E **S** T Y
5   P E R F **O** R M A N C E
6   D E P E **N** D A B L E
7   L O Y **A** L T Y
8   H E A **L** T H
9   P U N C **T** U A L
10   C O U **R** T E S Y
11   **A** T T I T U D E
12   I N I T **I** A T I V E
13 W O R K E **T** H I C
14 S E L F – E **S** T E E M

Definitions:

1. To be accountable

2. How you look

3. To get along with your coworkers and supervisor

4. Integrity; being truthful

5. To put forth your best effort and do a job well

6. Someone who is reliable

7. Being faithful to your employer

8. Mental and physical condition

9. Being on time

10. Showing good manners

11. An outlook on life

12. Finding tasks to do without being told

13. How much effort you put into your work

14. How you see yourself

Dependability and Work Ethic

Activity D   Name _____

Chapter 3   Date _____ Period _____

Read the following story about Joseph. Then answer the questions below.

    Joseph was hired by Mr. Johnson as a stocker in a grocery store. His job responsibilities included unloading boxes from delivery trucks and stocking the store shelves, refrigerators, and freezers. One Tuesday morning, Joseph unloaded some boxes of frozen food products from a delivery truck, but didn't follow his employer's directions to transfer the food to the freezer quickly. Mr. Johnson had explained that frozen food cannot be allowed to thaw. Joseph, however, became distracted by some of his friends who came to the store to talk with him. At noon, Joseph was hungry so he left for lunch without asking permission. He decided to handle important personal business instead of returning to work that afternoon. When Joseph arrived at work Wednesday morning, he was surprised to learn that Mr. Johnson had fired him and hired a replacement.

1. Was Mr. Johnson justified in firing Joseph? Explain. (Sample response.) Yes. Joseph didn't follow
   Mr. Johnson's directions. He allowed food to become ruined. He talked to his friends on work time and
   then left work early.
   _____
   _____
   _____

2. If you were Mr. Johnson, what would you have said to Joseph on Wednesday? (Sample response.) I can't
   count on you to follow directions, and you don't show a strong work ethic. You cost me money by allowing
   the food to thaw and be ruined.
   _____
   _____
   _____

3. What should Joseph have done about his friends distracting him from his work? (Sample response.) He
   should have told them to leave and he would call them later, after work.
   _____
   _____
   _____
   _____

4. What should Joseph have done about his personal business? (Sample response.) Joseph should not have
   left work. He should have taken care of personal business on his own time.
   _____
   _____
   _____
   _____

Employer Job Evaluation

Activity E

Chapter 3

Name_____

Date_____Period_____

Evaluate your job performance from the viewpoint of an employer by placing a check in the appropriate spaces. Then answer the questions that follow. (Answers are student response.)

1. Cooperation

_____ A Gets along well with others; is friendly with others.
_____ B Cooperates willingly; gets along with others.
_____ C Usually gets along with others.
_____ D Does not work well with others.
_____ E Is antagonistic; pulls against rather than works with others.

2. Initiative

_____ A Is resourceful; looks for tasks to learn and do.
_____ B Is fairly resourceful; does well by himself/herself.
_____ C Does routine work acceptably.
_____ D Takes very little initiative; requires urging.
_____ E Takes no initiative; has to be instructed repeatedly.

3. Courtesy

_____ A Is very courteous and very considerate of others.
_____ B Is considerate and courteous.
_____ C Usually is polite and considerate of others.
_____ D Is not particularly courteous in action or speech.
_____ E Has been discourteous to the public and staff.

4. Attitude Toward Constructive Criticism

_____ A Accepts criticism and improves greatly.
_____ B Accepts criticism and improvement noted.
_____ C Accepts criticism and tries to do better.
_____ D Doesn't pay much attention to criticism.
_____ E Doesn't profit by criticism; resents it.

5. Knowledge of Job

_____ A Knows job well and shows desire to learn more.
_____ B Understands work; needs little supervision.
_____ C Has learned necessary routine but needs supervision.
_____ D Pays little attention to learning job.
_____ E Has not tried to learn.

6. Accuracy of Work

_____ A Very seldom makes errors; does work of very good quality.
_____ B Makes few errors; is careful, thorough, and neat.
_____ C Makes errors; shows average care, thoroughness, and neatness.
_____ D Is frequently inaccurate and careless.
_____ E Is extremely careless.

7. Work Accomplished

_____ A Is fast and efficient; production is well above average.
_____ B Works rapidly; output is above average.
_____ C Works with ordinary speed; work is generally satisfactory.
_____ D Is slower than average.
_____ E Is very slow; output is unsatisfactory.

(Continued)

8. Work Habits

_____ A Is industrious; concentrates very well.
_____ B Seldom wastes time; is reliable.
_____ C Wastes time occasionally; is usually reliable.
_____ D Frequently wastes time; needs close supervision.
_____ E Habitually wastes time; has to be watched and reminded of work.

9. Adaptability

_____ A Learns quickly; is adept at meeting changing conditions.
_____ B Adjusts readily.
_____ C Makes necessary adjustments after considerable instruction.
_____ D Is slow in grasping ideas; has difficulty adapting to new situations.
_____ E Can't adjust to changing situations.

10. Personal Appearance

_____ A Is excellent in appearance; always looks neat.
_____ B Is very good in appearance; looks neat most of the time.
_____ C Is passable in appearance but should make effort to improve.
_____ D Often neglects appearance.
_____ E Is extremely careless in appearance.

11. Punctuality

_____ A Never tardy except for unavoidable emergencies.
_____ B Seldom tardy.
_____ C Punctuality could be improved.
_____ D Very often tardy.
_____ E Too frequently tardy.

12. Dependability

_____ A Never absent except for an unavoidable emergency.
_____ B Dependable.
_____ C Usually dependable.
_____ D Not regular enough in attendance.
_____ E Too frequently absent.

1. Do you believe this is an accurate evaluation of your work habits and performance? Explain. _____
   (Student response.)
   _____

2. In which areas could you improve? Explain. (Student response.) _____
   _____

3. Which areas are your strongest? Why? (Student response.) _____
   _____

4. Based on this evaluation, do you think you are a desirable employee? Explain. (Student response.) _____
   _____
   _____

5. In your opinion, what are three cases of employee absence that deserve to be excused? _____
   (Student response.)
   _____

Teamwork and Problem-Solving Skills

Handling Problems in Teams

Activity A

Chapter 4

Name _____

Date _____ Period _____

Effective teams work together to address problems that occur among members. In order to keep a team working effectively, what would you say or do to a team member in the following situations?

Problem Behavior

What would you say or do?

1. Is always late.

   (Sample response.) Remind the person that the meeting starts promptly at the arranged time.

2. Frequently starts side conversations during discussions.

   (Sample response.) Ask the person privately to stop distracting others.

3. Acts offended if his or her recommendations are not followed.

   (Sample response.) Remind the person all team members make valuable contributions.

4. Rushes through to a quick decision to end a discussion.

   (Sample response.) Remind everyone that decisions take careful consideration.

5. Monopolizes the discussion.

   (Sample response.) Ask specifically for input from others.

6. Leaves before the job is done.

   (Sample response.) Remind the person that everyone's contribution is needed to complete a project.

7. Brings personal problems to work.

   (Sample response.) Express sympathy, but ask the person to focus when necessary.

8. Constantly tells jokes and keeps the team from working.

   (Sample response.) Tell the person that humor is appropriate only in moderation.

9. Refuses to work with another team member.

   (Sample response.) Mediate between the team members to clear up problems.

10. Gives lengthy, time-wasting explanations.

    (Sample response.) Ask for more succinct, direct answers.

11. Suddenly turns silent.

    (Sample response.) Ask later if anything is wrong.

12. Won't share the leadership role.

    (Sample response.) Remind the person that everyone has strengths and weaknesses that can benefit the team.

Using a Chart as a Scheduling Tool

Activity B

Chapter 4

Name_____

Date_____ Period_____

Working in a team, plan the fund-raising event described below. Then use the chart outline at the bottom of the page to develop a Gantt chart for planning, executing, and evaluating the fund-raiser. If necessary, refer to the Gantt chart in your text.

"Spring Break" T-Shirt Fund-Raising Event: Imagine that your group is the club committee responsible for the entire fund-raising event. Your club advisor has instructed that the fund-raiser—from start to finish—should take no more than eight weeks. During that period, your team must create the shirt's design; find a shirt manufacturer and select colors; find a printer; determine production costs and selling price; take orders; collect money; and distribute the shirts. Your committee, as well as all other club members, will sell the T-shirts during a two-week period. After the sales period, you must finalize financial records and give a report to your club. (Sample response.)

Planning Guide for T-Shirt Fund-Raising

Task	Week 1	Week 2	Week 3	Week 4	Week 5	Week 6	Week 7	Week 8
Create design	▓							
Find a manufacturer and select colors	▓	▓						
Find a printer		▓	▓					
Determine production costs and selling price			▓	▓				
Take orders					▓	▓		
Collect money					▓	▓		
Distribute shirts					▓	▓		
Finalize financial records							▓	▓
Give a report to the club								▓

Let's Work as a Team

Activity C

Chapter 4

Name _____

Date _____ Period _____

Work with three or four classmates to develop a car-buying chart as described below. Begin the group project by establishing team roles and brainstorming how to set up the chart. As a group, present your completed chart to the class. Work alone to answer the questions that follow.

Team Project: Creating a Car-Buying Guide

Assume your team works in a car-buying assistance department of a large travel club. Customers call your information line for help in deciding which new vehicles to purchase. Your department manager has asked your team to help this decision-making process by designing a chart that shows the following categories:

- types of vehicles available, such as compact/small, medium, large/luxury, minivans, sport-utility vehicles, convertibles, and pickups
- important buying information, such as safety features, miles-per-gallon rating, price ranges, equipment options, seating capacity, special awards, and results of collision tests
- other information your team feels is valuable

Research the information needed by checking consumer magazines, buying guides, newspapers, car specialty magazines, and the Internet. Design the chart on a large piece of paper or poster board. Indicate what types of pictures should be shown where.

---

1. What occurred among the members of your team during the following stages?

   A. Forming stage: (Student response.) _____

   _____

   _____

   _____

   B. Storming stage: (Student response.) _____

   _____

   _____

   _____

   C. Norming stage: (Student response.) _____

   _____

   _____

   _____

   D. Performing stage: (Student response.) _____

   _____

   _____

   _____

(Continued)

Name_____

2. Which team members fit each of the following roles?

Leader(s): (Student response.) _____

_____

_____

Encourager(s): (Student response.) _____

_____

_____

Taskmaster(s): (Student response.) _____

_____

_____

Critic(s): (Student response.) _____

_____

_____

Recorder: (Student response.) _____

_____

_____

3. How did your team resolve any disagreements that occurred?

(Student response.) _____

_____

_____

_____

4. Which characteristics of an effective team developed within your group during the project?

(Student response.) _____

_____

_____

_____

5. What ideas resulted from the group's brainstorming sessions?

(Student response.) _____

_____

_____

_____

Team Problem-Solving Case Study

Activity D

Chapter 4

Name _____

Date _____ Period _____

In teams of five, review the following case study. Then use the problem-solving steps that follow to assist your team and solve the problem.

Case Study: World Class Café, a restaurant specializing in international cuisine, seats 70 customers. It is open every day for lunch and dinner. Weekend nights are always busy, with the wait time often being an hour. Many of the customers are repeat customers. On a typical weekend night, the front room is fully staffed with one hostess, five waiters, and two busers. There is one manager on duty for both the front room and the kitchen areas.

This Saturday night, a nearby company has reserved half the seats for a party from 6 p.m. to 9 p.m. On Thursday, two waiters and one buser have notified the manager that they cannot work this weekend. The manager calls a meeting of the front-room staff to develop a Saturday action plan for the work team. The front-room staff must address the staffing problem and be prepared to handle possible complaints about prices, food quality, and/or service.

Step 1: Identify and analyze the problem.

What is the problem?

There will not be enough staff to handle the usual weekend crowd plus the special party on Saturday.

_____

_____

What criteria would you consider?

(Sample response.) Complaints will have to be handled gracefully. Service will have to be good enough to

not alienate regular customers.

_____

_____

What constraints would you consider?

(Sample response.) There is a large party from 6 p.m. to 9 p.m. The team will be down three staff members.

The staff has only two days to make a plan.

_____

_____

Step 2: Collect and analyze data.

What do you need to know about the problem that you do not already know?

(Sample response.) Will management consider comping customers with free items or gift certificates for

future visits? Can kitchen staff or hostess double as wait staff? Can wait staff do their own busing?

_____

What information is available to you to help you solve this problem?

(Sample response.) There are regularly five waiters and two busers. Half the seats will be taken up by one

party.

(Continued)

Name_____

Step 3: Consider possible solutions.

What are some possible solutions developed by your team through brainstorming?

(Student response.)

_____

_____

_____

_____

_____

_____

_____

_____

Step 4: Choose the best plan.

Considering your answers in Step 1, which plan seems best?

(Student response.)

_____

_____

_____

_____

Step 5: Implement the plan.

What clues might indicate that the plan is (is not) working?

(Sample response.) Customers are angry. Customers are not receiving service or food. In the next few

weeks, customers may not return.

_____

_____

_____

Step 6: Observe, evaluate, and adjust.

If this plan fails, what would your team recommend doing next time?

(Student response.)

_____

_____

_____

What aids to problem solving did your team use? Give details.

(Student response.)

_____

_____

_____

_____

Teamwork and Problem-Solving Terms

Activity E

Chapter 4

Name_____

Date_____ Period_____

Match the following chapter terms with their definitions by writing the correct letter in each blank. Then answer the questions that follow.

___F___ 1. A cross-trained group that has all members able to perform all duties.

___I___ 2. The stage of team development when individuals are first grouped together.

___B___ 3. What a company tries to achieve by meeting and exceeding customer expectations.

___E___ 4. A team that has full responsibility for carrying out its assignment.

___Q___ 5. When all members of a group fully accept and support a decision.

___K___ 6. The highest stage of team development.

___D___ 7. A team consisting of workers from different areas who are grouped together to work on a specific project.

___M___ 8. The process of making an expectation a reality.

___O___ 9. Factors that may restrict your ability to solve a problem.

___G___ 10. A pattern that is typical in the development of a social group.

___R___ 11. A hostile situation resulting from opposing views.

___H___ 12. A timetable graph used to help teams stay focused.

___J___ 13. The stage of team development where disagreements are likely to occur.

___C___ 14. A team with members of similar skills who are not able to perform one another's jobs.

___P___ 15. A group technique used to develop many ideas in a short time.

___N___ 16. The standards you use to find the best solution in problem solving.

___A___ 17. A small group of people working together for a common purpose.

___L___ 18. The objective that you want to attain.

A. team
B. quality
C. functional team
D. cross-functional team
E. self-directed team
F. multifunctional team
G. norm
H. Gantt chart
I. forming stage
J. storming stage
K. performing stage
L. goal
M. problem solving
N. criteria
O. constraints
P. brainstorming
Q. consensus
R. conflict

19. What does *working for a common good* mean? _working toward a goal that is considered the best overall_

_____

_____

20. When is humor beneficial to a team? _when it relaxes team members and helps them focus on issues_

_____

(Continued)

Name_____

21. What methods could a team use to stay focused on its mission? <u>Use humor effectively; takes breaks;</u>
<u>list goals.</u>
_____
_____

22. What example of team conflict have you witnessed? (How was it resolved?) <u>(Student response.)</u>
_____
_____
_____

23. What could have been done differently by the team described in Item 22 to prevent team conflict?_____
<u>(Student response.)</u>
_____
_____

24. For the teams on which you have served, what roles did the teams play? (Indicate below)
(Student response.)

Team Name/Description	Functional	Cross-Functional	Self-Directed	Multifunctional
At school:_____	☐	☐	☐	☐
_____	☐	☐	☐	☐
At work: _____	☐	☐	☐	☐
_____	☐	☐	☐	☐
In sports: _____	☐	☐	☐	☐
_____	☐	☐	☐	☐
Other/volunteer: _____	☐	☐	☐	☐
_____	☐	☐	☐	☐

 # Communicating on the Job

Effective Communication

Effective communication skills are necessary in the workplace and will improve your job performance. Prepare a written message in a word processing program and exchange your message with a partner. Then evaluate your own communication skills by answering the questions below. Share the evaluation with the class.

1. Who was the sender of the message? _me_____

2. What was the encoder? _my mind_____

3. What was the message? (Student response.)_____

4. What was the channel? _word processing program_____

5. Who was the receiver? (Student response.)_____

6. What was the decoder? _the receiver's mind_____

7. Was there any feedback? _____ If so, what was it? (Student response.)_____

_____

8. Was there any noise? _____ If so, what was it? (Student response.)_____

_____

9. Did effective communication occur? _____ Why or why not? (Student response.)_____

_____

10. Based on your answers to these questions, describe yourself as a communicator. (Student response.)_____

_____

_____

_____

_____

11. What can you do to become a more effective communicator? (Student response.)_____

_____

_____

_____

_____

How Well Do You Listen?

Activity B

Chapter 5

Name_____

Date _____ Period _____

How well do you listen? Think about the conversations you have with others, including family members, teachers, and friends. Respond to the following statements by checking the response that best describes your behavior. Then analyze your responses. (Answers are student response.)

Often	Sometimes	Never	
_____	_____	_____	1. Are you distracted by others talking nearby?
_____	_____	_____	2. Do you continue to listen even though you think you know what is going to be said?
_____	_____	_____	3. Do you continue to listen even when you disagree with what is said?
_____	_____	_____	4. Do you have difficulty hearing the speaker?
_____	_____	_____	5. Does a speaker who does not make eye contact distract you?
_____	_____	_____	6. Do you continue to listen even though the speaker uses words you do not understand?
_____	_____	_____	7. Does your mind wander during a conversation?
_____	_____	_____	8. Do you interrupt others while they are talking?
_____	_____	_____	9. Do you ask the speaker to explain things you do not understand?
_____	_____	_____	10. Do you have trouble listening when others speak?

Based on your answers to these questions, describe yourself as a listener. _____

_____

_____

_____

_____

_____

_____

_____

Describe your major concerns about your listening skills. _____

_____

_____

_____

_____

_____

_____

Parts of Business Letters

Name_____

Date_____Period_____

Identify the eight standard parts indicated on the business letter below.

A

H. B. Jones Welding
812 N. 7th Avenue
Kansas City, Missouri 65100

B

November 15, 20xx

C

Acme Welding Supply
999 Camden St.
St. Louis, MO 63000

D

Dear Sir or Madam:

E

Please send me information about the new Acme welding machines you advertised in the *Welding Journal* last
month. My company rebuilds heavy road construction
equipment, and we need to replace five of our welding
machines.

If you have a salesperson in the Kansas City area, we
would appreciate having him or her call on us.

F

Sincerely,

G

Jackie Jones

Jackie Jones
Purchaser

H

JRJ/ra

A. return address _____

    _____

B. date _____

C. inside address _____

    _____

D. salutation _____

E. body _____

F. complimentary close _____

G. signature, printed name,

    and business title _____

H. reference initials _____

    _____

Complete the following statement: Neatness is important when writing a business letter because _____
(Sample response.) Neatness helps ensure that the message is conveyed clearly. A business letter that is messy
will not be taken seriously by the business that receives it.
_____
_____
_____

Writing a Business Letter

Activity D   Name_____

Chapter 5   Date_____Period_____

In the space below, write a letter ordering two sweaters from Sunrise Clothing Store, 123 Main Street, Clinton, Iowa 51030. The catalog order number is SW056. Use block style.   (Sample response.)

(Student address)

(Date)

Sunrise Clothing Store
123 Main Street
Clinton, Iowa 51030

To Whom It May Concern:

I would like to place an order from your most recent catalog. I would like to order two (2) sweaters, catalog number SW056. My check is included. I look forward to receiving my sweaters soon.

Sincerely,

(Student signature)

(Student name)

Combining Good and Bad News

Activity E

Chapter 5

Name _____

Date _____ Period _____

Imagine you work for Sunrise Clothing Store, a mail order business. Prepare a bad-news letter in response to the following letter. Enter your letter into a word processing document. Use modified block style. Be sure to include each of the eight standard parts of the business letter. In the box below, prepare an envelope for your letter with a return address.

Route 1
Clinton, Iowa 51030
February 22, 20xx

Manager
Sunrise Clothing Store
123 Main Street
Clinton, Iowa 51303

Dear Sir or Madam:

I recently bought two sweaters from your store. After washing one sweater, it shrank. Now the sweater is too small, and I can't wear it. It also changed color. I would like to return both sweaters and get my money back. Should I mail both of them to you?

Sincerely,

Martha Greenwell

Martha Greenwell

(Student's return address)

Martha Greenwell
Route 1
Clinton, Iowa 51030

Writing Memos

Name_____

Date_____Period_____

Imagine you are a supervisor at the King Manufacturing Company. As a supervisor, you must inform the workers in your section about a meeting that is to take place next Wednesday at 10:00 a.m. The purpose of the meeting is to explain new safety policies to all employees. The meeting will be held in the company's lunchroom where coffee, soft drinks, and doughnuts will be served. Using the form below, prepare a memo to the employees in your section.

King Manufacturing Company

MEMO

(Sample response.)

DATE: (Current date)

TO: All Employees

FROM: (Student name)

SUBJECT: Safety Policy Meeting

All employees are requested to attend a meeting in the company lunchroom next Wednesday at 10:00 a.m. We will be discussing new safety policies. Coffee, soft drinks, and doughnuts will be available.

Telephone Skills

Activity G   Name_____

Chapter 5   Date_____Period_____

Work with a partner to role-play the following situation. Have your partner imagine calling the law firm of Entis, Entis, and Martinez to arrange an interview for a school project. Role-play the part of the receptionist and ask if you can take a message for Ms. Entis, who is not available to take the call. Use the form below to take the message, then switch roles with your partner and repeat the role-play. Evaluate your partner's telephone skills by answering the questions below. (Sample response.)

To _Ms. Entis_____

Date _(Current date)_____ Time_(Current time)____

TELEPHONE MESSAGE/WHILE YOU WERE OUT

M _(Student response.)_____

of _(Student response.)_____

Phone _(Student response.)_____

[X] Telephoned   [X] Will call again

[ ] Returned your call   [ ] Called to see you

[ ] Please call   [ ] Wants to see you

Message _Would like to arrange an interview for a school_____

project._____

_____

_____

_____

_____

Message taken by _(Student response.)_____

---

1. Was the call answered immediately? _(Student response.)_____

2. Was the caller greeted pleasantly? _(Student response.)_____

3. Was the voice clear and distinct? _(Student response.)_____

4. Was proper grammar used? _(Student response.)_____

5. Was the message read back to the caller? _(Student response.)_____

6. Did the message contain all the key facts? _(Student response.)_____

Your Speaking Skills

Activity H	Name_____
Chapter 5	Date_____ Period_____

Imagine you are a school news reporter on special assignment for a local television station. Your assignment is to prepare a 90-second news report entitled "Work-Based Learning at (Your School)." Plan your report to cover the most important facts. (You may wish to report on class assignments, class activities, and jobs.) On another sheet of paper, write a brief outline of your report.

Present your report to the class, making sure it is 90-seconds long. (If possible, have your report video recorded or audiotaped.) Ask class members to evaluate you according to the six areas listed below. Then answer the following questions by summarizing their evaluations and evaluating yourself.

1. Speaking rate: (Student response.) _____
   _____

2. Eye contact: (Student response.) _____
   _____

3. Proper use of English: (Student response.) _____
   _____

4. Clear and distinct speech: (Student response.) _____
   _____

5. Nonverbal communication: (Student response.) _____
   _____

6. Other comments: (Student response.) _____
   _____

Based on the evaluations given by class members, how would you rate yourself as a speaker?_____
(Student response.) _____
_____
_____

What are your weaknesses as a speaker? (Student response.) _____
_____
_____
_____

How can you improve as a speaker? (Student response.) _____
_____
_____
_____

What are your strengths as a speaker? (Student response.) _____
_____

Math in the Workplace

Making Change

Name_____

Date_____Period_____

1. Suppose you work in a grocery store and a customer gives you a $20 bill for a $5.47 purchase. The total amount of change you should hand back is $ _14.53_. In the space provided below, write what you would say as you make change for the customer.

   "$5.47 and 3 cents (the pennies) equals $5.50…and 50 cents (two quarters) equals $6.00…and 4 dollars

   (four one-dollar bills) equals $10.00…and 10 dollars (a ten-dollar bill) equals $20."

   _____

   _____

   _____

   _____

   _____

   _____

   _____

   _____

   _____

   _____

   _____

   _____

2. Work with a partner to calculate the amount of change for each of the transactions below. Then practice counting back the change to each other.

Purchase Price	Amount Tendered	Change
$ 4.23	Ten-dollar bill	$5.77
$10.34	A ten and a five-dollar bill	$4.66
$ 1.55	Five-dollar bill	$3.45
$11.75	Twenty-dollar bill	$8.25
$ 2.16	Three one-dollar bills	$.84
$ 7.45	Fifty-dollar bill	$42.55

Using a Calculator

Activity B

Chapter 6

Name_____

Date_____ Period_____

Use a calculator to solve these math problems. If necessary, review the procedure in the text describing how to operate a calculator. Round off answers to the nearest hundredths.

Addition:

1.   75
     69
+ 34
  178
	2. 204
	    389
	+ 756
	  1,349
		3. 248.70
		  684.38
		+ 193.95
		 1,127.03
			4. 1,643.50
			 2,978.32
			+ 4,859.18
			  9,481

Subtraction:

5.   196
– 28
 168
	6. 2,487
	– 1,598
	   889
		7. 1,369.00
		– 951.83
		  417.17
			8. 16,874
			– 13,928
			  2,946

Multiplication:

9. 603 × 86 51,858	10. 1,936 × 367 710,512	11. 769 × .29 223.01	12. 14,792 × 49 724,808

Division:

13. $1{,}204 \div 28 =$ _43_____

14. $15{,}675 \div 57 =$ _275_____

15. $2{,}878.40 \div 67 =$ _42.96_____

16. $45{,}938 \div 340 =$ _135.11_____

Fractions, Decimals, and Percentages

Activity C

Chapter 6

Name_____

Date_____Period_____

Write the way you would read the common fractions below.

1. 4/10 _four-tenths_____

2. 5/16 _five-sixteenths_____

3. 18/27 _eighteen twenty-sevenths_____

4. 11/22 _eleven twenty-seconds_____

5. 3/5 _three-fifths_____

6. 125/300 _one-hundred twenty-five_____
   _____three-hundredths_____

Write the way you would read the decimal fractions below.

7. 0.075 _seventy-five thousandths_____

8. 0.95 _ninety-five hundredths_____

9. 0.6 _six-tenths_____

10. 0.5621 _five-thousand six-hundred twenty-one_
    _____ten-thousandths_____

11. 0.55 _fifty-five hundredths_____

12. 0.9 _nine-tenths_____

13. 0.0088 _eighty-eight ten-thousandths___

14. 0.634 _six-hundred thirty-four thousandths___

Change the following fractions into decimals. Round off to the nearest hundredth.

15. 25/75 _0.33_____

16. 4/5 _0.8_____

17. 7/4 _1.75_____

18. 125/100 _1.25_____

19. 11/22 _0.5_____

20. 16/64 _0.25_____

Calculate the answer for the following problems. Round off to the nearest hundredth.

21. If the sales tax rate in your state is 6½%, what is the tax on your purchase of shoes costing $22.99? _$1.49_

22. If the profit on a car priced at $12,350 is 15%, how much will the seller make? _$1,852.50_

23. If the discount on a computer costing $1,500 is 25%, what is the amount of the discount? _$375_

24. If the unemployment rate in your state is 3½% and there are 2,500,000 employable people in your state, how many people are unemployed? _87,500_

Taking Measurements

Activity D

Chapter 6

Name_____

Date_____Period_____

Using a ruler, draw lines of the following lengths:

1. ¾ inch

2. 3 inches

3. 1¼ inches

4. 2⅜ inches

5. 3½ inches

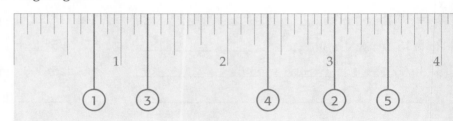

Measure length and width of this card:

6. Length: _3⅜ in._____ Width: _2⅛ in._____

Use a ruler or tape measure to measure the following items: (Answers 8–10 are student response.)

	Length	Width	Height (or thickness)
7. Workbook for *From School to Work*	11 in.	8 1/2 in.	1/2 in.
8. The dimensions of your classroom			
9. The door of your classroom			
10. The classroom's board			
11. One-dollar bill (U.S.)	6 1/8 in.	1 5/8 in.	N/A

Find the area of the geometric shapes shown below.

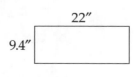

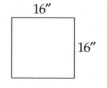

12. _206.8 sq. in._____   13. _256 sq. in._____   14. _24 sq. ft._____   15. _50.24 sq. in._____

Working with Metrics

Activity E

Chapter 6

Name_____

Date_____ Period_____

Answer the following questions using the metric conversion chart in the text on page 133.

___354.84 mm___ 1. Tanisha drank 12 ounces of milk. How many milliliters of milk did she drink?

___104.65 km per hour___ 2. The speed limit is 65 miles per hour. What is the speed limit in kilometers per hour?

___91 m___ 3. The length of a football field is 100 yards. What is the length in meters?

___49.5 kg___ 4. Sue weighs 110 pounds. What is her weight in kilograms?

___10.4 gal.___ 5. Manuel bought 40 liters of gasoline. How many gallons did he buy?

___86°F___ 6. The temperature is 30 degrees Celsius. What is the temperature in degrees Fahrenheit?

___20.32×25.4 cm___ 7. Ira bought a picture frame that is 8×10 inches. What is the size of the frame in centimeters?

___5.005 m___ 8. Cindy needs 5½ yards of fabric to cover a chair. How many meters of fabric does she need?

___38.08°C___ 9. Lei's body temperature is 100 degrees Fahrenheit. What is her temperature in degrees Celsius?

___186 miles___ 10. The distance from Tampa to Miami is 300 kilometers. What is the distance in miles?

___156 in.___ 11. The width of Jeff's room is 400 centimeters. How wide is the room in inches?

___13.76 oz.___ 12. Chun bought a steak weighing 344 grams. How many ounces does the steak weigh?

___0.95 l___ 13. Sara bought a quart of orange juice. How many liters of orange juice did she buy?

___39.36 ft.___ 14. The length of a swimming pool is 12 meters. What is the length in feet?

Analyzing Data

Activity F

Chapter 6

Name_____

Date_____Period_____

Analyze the chart to answer the first four questions. Then match the following chapter terms with their descriptions by writing the correct letter in each blank.

Atlantic Accounting Company		
Salary	**Number of Employees**	**Salary × Number**
$75,000	2 (5+ yrs. of service)	$150,000
$60,000	3 (2-5 yrs. of service)	$180,000
$42,000	4 (2-15 mos. of service)	$168,000
Total	9	$498,000

1. What is the mean salary? $59,000

2. What is the mode of the salaries? $42,000 (occurs four times)

3. What is the median of the salaries? $60,000

4. To a job applicant, which average is of greatest importance? $42,000 because it is the mean average of salaries for the newer employees

	Description	**Chart Name**
D	5. A fraction with a denominator (or multiple) of 10.	A. bar graph
G	6. Arranges data in rows and columns.	B. circle graph
E	7. Shows the relationship of two or more variables.	C. common fraction
A	8. Shows comparisons between categories.	D. decimal fraction
B	9. Shows the relationship of parts to the whole.	E. line graph
F	10. Presents information with the use of eye-catching images.	F. pictograph
		G. table

Technology and You

Computer Hardware

Name_____

Date_____Period_____

Complete the following statements by filling in the blanks.

_____laptop_____ 1. A lightweight, portable computer the size of a notebook is a _____.

_____hardware_____ 2. The physical equipment used in computer systems is the _____.

_____processor_____ 3. The central processing unit (CPU), also called the _____, controls what is done with the data received by the computer.

_____Random Access_____ 4. The amount of _____ _____ Memory on a computer affects how quickly it processes and runs programs.

_____graphics_____ 5. A video card helps the computer process complex _____, such as those found on the Internet and in games.

_____hard disk_____ 6. The internal _____ _____ drive of a computer stores the data to operate the computer, as well as all information entered by the user.

_____storage_____ 7. Writable CDs, DVDs and USB flash drives are all examples of _____ devices.

_____network_____ 8. Multiple computer terminals that can share information are linked through a closed _____.

_____server_____ 9. A _____ is a computer with extensive memory that is connected to other computers and allows businesses to regularly back up information.

_____management_____ 10. Keeping your files organized and easily retrievable on the computer is accomplished by using good file_____.

_____Peripherals_____ 11. _____ are any output and input devices that are plugged into a computer's CPU.

_____scanner_____ 12. A device that passes an electron beam over an image, allowing the image to be stored in the computer's memory, is called a _____.

_____compact flash_____ 13. Photos taken by a digital camera are saved on _____ _____ cards instead of film.

_____input_____ 14. Keyboards, mice, scanners, digital cameras, and webcams are all examples of _____ devices.

_____output_____ 15. Monitors and printers are examples of _____ devices.

_____webcams_____ 16. Cameras that are plugged into a computer and used to transmit videos to the Internet are called _____.

Investigating Web Sites

Activity B

Chapter 7

Name_____

Date _____ Period_____

Web sites are maintained by educational institutions, companies, organizations, government agencies, and individuals. It is important to be able to evaluate Web sites for credibility, accuracy, and timely information. Use a search engine to gather information about the key word *copyright*. Choose one Web address returned and evaluate the site using the following questions. Compare your findings with classmates. (Answers are student response.)

Search engine used: _____

URL of the Web site: _____

Who created the Web site?

What does the domain extension of the page (.gov, .edu, .com, .org) tell about the site?

When was the Web site last updated?

Where do links from this Web site take you?

How do you know this Web site is credible?
- Is the content accurate and objective?

- Is a bibliography of sources included?

- Is contact information available?

- Are the spelling and grammar correct?

- Does the information appear biased?

- Do pictures, photographs, and graphics add to the information?

List several key points of information you discovered about copyrights from this Web site:

✓

✓

✓

Essential Technology Skills Self-Check

Activity C   Name_____

Chapter 7   Date _____Period_____

Being familiar with computer technology is crucial for job success. Reflect on your skills for using technology by completing the self-assessment. (Self-assessment is student response.)

Computer Hardware Skills	Have	Need
1. Identify parts of a computer system including CPU, keyboard, monitor, mouse, speakers, printer, ports, and CD-ROM drive		
2. Set up new computer, connecting peripheral equipment		
3. Adjust display settings		
4. Insert, access, and eject a CD and/or USB flash drive		
5. Install new software and application		
6. Add memory to central processing unit (CPU)		
7. Transfer pictures/video from a digital camera or other media devices		
8. Scan a document and store as a file		
9. Determine available space on a drive/file/directory		
10. Troubleshoot problems, including memory and program compatibility		
11. Install/maintain virus protection and check for viruses		
12. Select and use printer; cancel print jobs		
General Computer Skills	**Have**	**Need**
13. Open programs and files		
14. Access help menus		
15. Navigate the desktop		
16. Resize and move windows and objects to new locations		
17. Navigate documents and dialog boxes by using vertical and horizontal scroll bars, mouse, directional arrows, and shortcut keys		
18. Customize menu and toolbars		
19. File management (locate, rename, and delete files, folders, and icons)		
20. Use directory structures to organize documents		
Computer Software Skills	**Have**	**Need**
21. Create, save, and print a word processing document		
22. Format text		
23. Edit by deleting, adding, and replacing characters and sections of text		
24. Cut/copy/paste text and objects into new locations		
25. Use of tool bars, spell check, print preview, search, and replace		
26. Draw a simple illustration using draw toolbars		
27. Create a spreadsheet using mathematical formulas and functions		
28. Import files into spreadsheets, databases, and/or word processing documents		
29. Sort data in a table and/or spreadsheet		
30. Create a database to store and retrieve records		
31. Create, edit, and produce a brochure or newsletter		
32. Create an electronic presentation/slide show		
Internet and E-Mail Skills	**Have**	**Need**
33. Connect to the Internet using a service provider		
34. Access a Web page by entering a URL, using a bookmark, or following a link		
35. Conduct Web searches using search engines		
36. Compose, address, and send e-mail		
37. Reply to and forward e-mail		
38. Add, open, and save attachments		
39. Print messages and attachments		
40. Create distribution lists		

The Impact of Technology

Activity D   Name _____

Chapter 7   Date _____ Period _____

Computers play an important part on the job, at school and in the home. List three ways computers are used in each area below. Then answer the questions that follow.   (List three for each:)

Technology on the job:

1. _____ (Sample response.) Web site to advertise and sell company products and/or services _____

2. _____ (Sample response.) conduct online research _____

3. _____ (Sample response.) globalization _____

Technology at school:

1. _____ (Sample response.) instructional purposes _____

2. _____ (Sample response.) accessing library resources _____

3. _____ (Sample response.) E-learning _____

Technology in the home:

1. _____ (Sample response.) communication _____

2. _____ (Sample response.) entertainment systems _____

3. _____ (Sample response.) banking _____

A. What types of technology have you used this past week? (Student response.) _____

_____

_____

_____

(Continued)

Name_____

B. How is technology used in your present job or at school? _(Student response.)_ _____

_____

_____

_____

C. What technology courses have you taken (keyboarding, software applications, desktop publishing, computer-aided drafting, programming, multimedia, etc.)? _(Student response.)_ _____

_____

_____

_____

D. What technology skills will be needed for employment in the future? _(Sample response.) basic_

knowledge of computers, keyboarding skills, knowledge of multimedia _____

_____

_____

E. How will technology affect the way you live and work in the next five years? _(Student response.)_

_____

Next ten years? _(Student response.)_ _____

_____

Next twenty years? _(Student response.)_ _____

_____

F. What emerging technology do you think will be in every automobile within the next five years?

(Sample response.) wireless technology, GPS navigation technology _____

_____

_____

Computer-Related Careers

Activity E
Chapter 7

Name_____

Date_____ Period_____

Match the following occupations to the appropriate job descriptions by writing the correct letter in each blank. Then answer the questions below.

___E___ 1. Writes a program to set up a payroll system.

___B___ 2. Repairs computer equipment.

___C___ 3. Links a company's manufacturing operations to automatic inventory control.

___F___ 4. Codes instructions for the tools used to cut metal sections for automobile parts.

___A___ 5. Performs routine computer operations in an office.

___D___ 6. Inputs data into a computer system.

___G___ 7. Creates and maintains a company's Web site.

A. computer operator
B. computer service technician
C. computer systems analyst
D. data entry keyer
E. software developer
F. tool programmer
G. Webmaster

8. Think of an occupation you might like to have in the future. Which technology applications would you use in that occupation? (Student response.)

_____

_____

_____

_____

_____

9. Where would you receive training to operate the technology? (Student response.)

_____

_____

_____

10. What jobs will be changed with the advancement of technology? (Answers may vary.) meter readers, bank tellers, travel agents

_____

_____

_____

Looking Good on the Job

MyPyramid Plan

Activity A

Chapter 8

Name_____

Date_____Period_____

Log on to the www.MyPyramid.gov Web site. Click on the subject *MyPyramid Plan*. Enter your age, gender, and physical activity to generate your personal MyPyramid plan. Print the PDF version of your results and use it to complete the chart below. (Chart answers are student response.)

Food Group	Recommended Amount
Grains	
Vegetables	
Fruits	
Milk	
Meat and beans	
Total calories	
Physical activity (minutes)	

Using foods and beverages typically available to you, plan a one-day menu that follows your personalized plan, including snacks. Use the Web site as a resource to help you determine the ounce-equivalents for grains and meat and beans. (Menus are student response.)

Breakfast menu:

_____

_____

_____

_____

Lunch menu:

_____

_____

_____

_____

Dinner menu:

_____

_____

_____

_____

Snacks menu:

_____

_____

_____

_____

(Continued)

Name_____

1. Did you eat the recommended servings from each food group? Explain. <u>(Student response.)</u>

   _____

   _____

   _____

   _____

   _____

   _____

2. How do the number and types of meals you eat every day affect how you feel? <u>(Sample response.)</u>
   <u>Eating nutritious meals and snacks regularly is the best way to maintain energy throughout the day and</u>
   <u>stay healthy.</u>

   _____

   _____

3. Why is it necessary to include sources from each food group in your daily diet? <u>Foods from each food</u>
   <u>group are needed to help supply your body with the daily nutrients it needs to develop and grow.</u>

   _____

   _____

4. Did you eat a variety of foods this day? Explain why or why not. <u>(Student response.)</u>

   _____

   _____

   _____

5. Of the foods you ate, which provided starch? <u>(Sample response.) breads, cereals, rice, pasta, potatoes</u>

   _____

6. Of the foods you ate, which provided fiber? <u>(Sample response.) whole grains, fruits, vegetables</u>

   _____

7. Did you limit your intake of foods containing fats, sugar, and sodium? <u>(Student response.)</u>

8. What steps can you take to improve your eating habits? <u>(Sample response.) eat recommended amounts</u>
   <u>of foods from each of the food groups; eat nutrient-dense foods that provide large amounts of vitamins</u>
   <u>and minerals; limit fats, sugar, and sodium; eat meals regularly; select nutritious snacks such as fruits or</u>
   <u>vegetables</u>

   _____

   _____

Exercise Regularly

Activity B   Name _____

Chapter 8   Date _____ Period _____

The chart below shows a good fitness plan for Jamie, a healthy teen of average height and weight. Using the information in the chart, answer the questions in the spaces provided.

Jamie's Fitness Plan

Type: Aerobic dancing
Place: Physical education class and aerobic dance classes
Time of day: During and after school
Duration: 40 minutes
Frequency: 5 times a week
Warm-up exercises: 5 minutes of leg stretches, toe touches, and limbering up body by slowly running in place to gradually increase heart circulation
Cool-down exercises: 5 minutes of slow running in place, then stress-reduction relaxation

---

1. How can Jamie benefit from exercising regularly? (Answers may vary.) improve heart and blood circulation, strengthen muscles, control weight, help relieve stress or tension

2. Why did Jamie incorporate warm-up and cool-down exercises into her fitness program? to give her
   body more time to adjust to the physical demands of the exercise

3. What exercises does Jamie do to develop her muscle strength, coordination, and flexibility? warm-up
   and cool-down stretches

4. Jamie chose aerobic dancing because she enjoys it. What other activities could Jamie do to exercise the
   heart and lungs? (Answers may vary.) walking briskly, bicycling, jogging, jumping rope, swimming,
   skiing

5. In the space below, make a fitness plan like Jamie's for yourself. (Sample response.)

   Type of activity: Jogging

   Place of activity: Park or indoor track

   Time of day: In the morning

   Activity duration: 40 minutes

   Activity frequency: 5–6 times a week

   Warm-up exercises: 5 minutes of calisthenics such as toe touches, body stretches, and jogging in place to
   increase heart circulation

   Cool-down exercises: 5 minutes of jogging in place, then light body stretches

Looking Good

Activity C
Chapter 8

Name_____

Date_____Period_____

Read the story about Ron. Then fill in the blanks to complete the following grooming tips that could help Ron improve his appearance.

Ron's Appearance

Ron seems to be a nice person, but people usually try to avoid him. He is not very clean, and his clothes never seem to look right on him. Ron probably was never taught to take care of his hair, clothes, and body. As a result, Ron does not look good on the job or at school.

---

1. Good _grooming_ is essential to getting and keeping a job.
2. Keeping the body clean is called good _hygiene_ .
3. Use a(n) _deodorant_ or _antiperspirant_ to help control body odor.
4. For the clean-shaven look, most men must _shave_ every day.
5. To maintain a beard or mustache, it should be neatly combed and _shaped_ .
6. Shaving under the arms can help reduce _perspiration_ odor.
7. To keep the skin free of bacteria, dirt, and oils, a person should _cleanse_ regularly with warm soapy water or a cleanser.
8. For problem skin, the person to see for help is a(n) _dermatologist_ .
9. Since your hair can greatly enhance your personal appearance, it is important to keep your hair _clean_ and _styled_ .
10. A(n) _hairstylist_ will be able to help you choose the best hair style for you.
11. Keep hands and fingernails clean and neatly _manicured_ .
12. For clean, healthy teeth and fresh breath, a person should _brush_ their teeth regularly.
13. A person is dressed right for the job if he or she wears clean clothes that fit properly and are _appropriate_ for the workplace.
14. A good way to decide what is best to wear to work is to know your company's _dress_ _code_ .
15. Caring for your clothes by keeping them clean, neatly pressed, and mended will help you have a(n) _attractive_ _appearance_ .

Appropriate Clothes for the Job

Activity D

Chapter 8

Name_____

Date_____Period_____

Answer the following questions about what clothes are appropriate for various types of jobs, including your job. Then discuss your answers with the class.

1. What clothes would be most appropriate if you worked

   A. in a bakery? clothes that can be cleaned easily, a hairnet may be needed

   B. as a construction worker? durable clothes or coveralls; safety clothing like a hard hat, safety shoes, and safety glasses

   C. in a child care center? nice slacks and shirt that can be cleaned easily

   D. as a receptionist in an office? females—nice slacks with a blouse or sweater; males—nice slacks with a shirt and tie

   E. as a clerk in a grocery store? nice slacks and shirt

   F. as an auto mechanic? durable clothes to withstand wear, tear, grease, and oil; coveralls

   G. as a computer analyst? females—nice slacks with a blouse or sweater; males—nice slacks with a shirt and tie

   H. as a medical technician? a uniform or lab coat that can be cleaned easily

   I. as a landscaper? durable clothes that will protect workers from the weather

   J. as a salesperson in a department store? females—nice slacks with a blouse or sweater; males—nice slacks with a shirt and tie

2. Name another job and describe the type of clothes appropriate for it.

   Job: (Sample response.) dental assistant

   Appropriate clothes: (Sample response.) a uniform or lab coat that can be cleaned easily

3. Describe the type of clothes appropriate to wear to your workplace.

   Job: (Student response.)

   Appropriate clothes: (Student response.)

Your Wardrobe

Activity E   Name_____

Chapter 8   Date_____ Period_____

Evaluate your wardrobe by following the steps below. (Answers 1–2 are student response.)

1. On a separate sheet of paper, prepare a wardrobe inventory. List all the clothes, shoes, and accessories you have for school, work, and other occasions. As you examine each item, decide whether you will keep (*K*), discard (*D*), or replace (*R*) it. Put the appropriate letter next to each item on your list.

2. Using your inventory, identify the gaps in your wardrobe. Review the items you want to replace and list them in the following chart. Then add the new items you want. Estimate the costs of new purchases, using information found on the Internet or a catalog for reference if necessary.

Wardrobe Planning		
Wardrobe Gaps	**Items Needed**	**Cost Estimates**
		Total

3. Describe how to care for your clothes properly. _remove clothes carefully; check clothes for stains, tears, and missing buttons; remove stains right away; put clothes away properly; when cleaning clothes, follow the directions on clothing care labels_

4. Identify factors important to dressing appropriately for the workplace._wear clean clothes; make sure your clothes fit properly and are appropriate for the work you will be doing; follow the company's dress code_

Safety on the Job

Job Safety Procedures

Activity A

Chapter 9

Name_____

Date_____Period_____

Interview a supervisor who is responsible for job safety procedures. Consult the employee handbook and answer the following questions.

1. Is your work site safe at all times? Explain. _(Student response.)_____

_____

_____

2. How do you maintain a safety-conscious attitude at all times? Explain. _(Sample response.) "think_

safety" by wearing proper clothing, using proper equipment, and following all safety procedures exactly

_____

3. What safety rules and regulations must you follow? _(Sample response.) All safety rules and regulations_

_in the handbook should be followed at all times._____

_____

4. What safety signs are posted at your work site? _(Student response.)_____

_____

5. What does your employee handbook say about safety? _(Student response.)_____

_____

6. What type of fire extinguisher is available? _(Answers will vary.) ordinary combustibles (A); flammable_

_liquids (B); electrical equipment (C); combustible metals (D)_____

_____

7. Where at your work site are the following located: fire extinguisher? fire alarm? emergency exits?_____

_(Student response.)_____

_____

8. Where are emergency phone numbers posted? _(Student response.)_____

_____

9. Are there pieces of equipment at your work site that some employees cannot legally operate because of age? Explain. _(Student response.)_____

_____

Protection from Environmental Hazards

Activity B   Name_____

Chapter 9   Date_____ Period_____

Match the environmental hazards with the proper protective clothing or device.

___G___ 1. High frequency sounds.

___H___ 2. Eye injuries.

___F___ 3. Welding burns.

___B___ 4. Harmful gases.

___A___ 5. Burns from flames and hot metal.

___C___ 6. Burns from acids, caustics, and alkalies.

___E___ 7. Cuts and abrasions on the hands.

___D___ 8. Injuries from falling objects.

A. asbestos gloves and leggings

B. masks and respirators

C. rubber gloves, aprons, and face shields

D. hard hats and safety shoes

E. gloves

F. leather gloves and apron shields

G. earplugs and earmuffs

H. safety goggles and face shields

Describe the environmental hazards (if any) that you might encounter on your job or at school. _(Sample response.) unsafe conditions involving heavy equipment, ladders, hand and power tools, electricity, or heights_

How can you protect yourself from these environmental hazards? _(Sample response.) Be safety-conscious. Know the hazards and take appropriate steps to avoid accidents._

What training in universal precautions should all workers receive? _Use protective barriers such as masks, gowns, gloves, and eye protection. Always wear latex gloves when handling blood. Dispose of gloves properly. Wash hands after handling blood even if gloves were worn. If blood has made contact with any part of the body, wash or rinse thoroughly and see a doctor immediately._

List the basic first aid steps to follow when a person is injured in an accident. _Remain calm. If possible, rescue the person from the hazardous situation. Do not move the person unless there is a threat of further injury. Make sure nothing is in the person's mouth or throat that could interfere with breathing. Stop any bleeding by applying pressure to the wound. Help to prevent shock by keeping the person warm and flat on his or her back with the head low. Call for medical help. Stay with the person until medical help arrives._

Accident Prevention

Activity C   Name_____
Chapter 9   Date_____ Period_____

Answer the following questions regarding safety at your workplace.   (Sample responses are shown.)
Your type of work: Receptionist
_____

Describe an accident that has occurred on the job, either to you or to someone else. Water was spilled on the
floor and not cleaned up, which caused a worker to fall.
_____
_____
_____

Explain how the accident could have been prevented. The spill should have been cleaned up immediately
and a sign posted to caution workers that the floor was wet.
_____
_____
_____

What safety procedures can you follow on the job to help prevent accidents? Do the job correctly. Think
and act safely. Avoid unsafe acts and correct unsafe working conditions. Know and follow safety rules and
precautions. Stay healthy. Use machines and tools properly. Use protective safety equipment when needed.
_____

What does your employer do to make the workplace safe? provides necessary training to workers; posts
safety signs and emergency numbers in a convenient location for all employees; conducts safety inspections
_____
_____

What type of safety training have you had on your present or former jobs? CPR, first aid, fire safety
_____
_____
_____

Why is it to your employer's advantage to promote safety at the workplace? The less injuries that occur in
the workplace will save an employer from losing time and money.
_____
_____
_____

Workplace Violence Awareness

Activity D

Chapter 9

Name_____

Date_____Period_____

For each statement below, circle *T* if it is true or *F* if it is false.

T (F) 1. Workplace violence is not a serious problem in America.

T (F) 2. Workplace violence is always a physical attack.

(T) F 3. Customers sometimes commit violence in the workplace.

(T) F 4. Robbery can be a motive for violence in the workplace.

(T) F 5. Workplace violence includes threatening behavior.

(T) F 6. A mentally unstable person may commit workplace violence because of an imagined problem.

T (F) 7. Pushing someone is not a physical act of violence.

(T) F 8. Swearing is a form of workplace violence.

T (F) 9. There is no need to alert your supervisor if you have safety concerns.

(T) F 10. A person who works alone has a greater chance of being a victim of workplace violence.

(T) F 11. Domestic problems can be a motive to commit workplace violence.

(T) F 12. Most murders in the workplace are connected to a robbery.

T (F) 13. Where you work is not an important factor in workplace violence.

T (F) 14. Retail businesses are less prone to workplace violence.

(T) F 15. Installing surveillance systems may help prevent workplace violence.

(T) F 16. A written threat is a psychological attack.

(T) F 17. Harassment is a form of psychological violence.

T (F) 18. Learning how to recognize potentially violent situations will not help prevent workplace violence.

Safety Committee Presentation

Activity E

Chapter 9

Name_____

Date_____Period_____

Imagine you are a member of a safety committee. Working with two or three classmates, choose one of the topics listed below and develop the topic into a presentation on workplace safety useful for staff training. Research current facts on the topic and learn about the latest technology and recommended procedures related to it. Make a group presentation to the class, reporting your findings and demonstrating any key procedures. Briefly outline your group's presentation below.

Choice of topics:

1. Fire and weather-warning safety, types and proper use of fire extinguishers, and evacuation procedures

2. Health safety, including first aid and universal precautions

3. Office safety, including ergonomics and air quality

4. Food service safety, including food handling procedures and proper use of machinery, cleaning agents, and protective clothing

5. Road-related safety, including vehicle maintenance and driver training and testing requirements

Presentation outline:

(Presentations will vary. Students' responses should reflect an understanding of workplace safety, accidents, causes, and prevention. Demonstrations should be utilized when appropriate. Information found in sources other than the text should be documented.)

_____

_____

_____

_____

_____

_____

_____

_____

_____

_____

_____

_____

_____

_____

_____

Protective Devices and Procedures

Activity F
Chapter 9

Name _____

Date _____ Period _____

For the occupations identified at the top of the chart, check the appropriate protective devices and procedures you would recommend to help workers avoid accidents on their jobs.

	Firefighter	Geologist	Welder	Airline Pilot	Surgeon	Salesclerk	Dental hygienist	Programmer	Auto technician	Coal miner	Your job
Devices:											
Leather gloves and apron			✓								
Gloves	✓				✓		✓				
Safety goggles and face shields		✓									
Hard hats and safety shoes	✓									✓	
Rubber gloves, aprons, face shields							✓				
Earplugs and earmuffs				✓							
Mask and respirator										✓	
Procedures:											
Conduct fire drills.	✓	✓	✓	✓	✓	✓	✓	✓	✓	✓	
Conduct random drug tests.	✓	✓	✓	✓	✓	✓	✓	✓	✓	✓	
Label and handle chemicals properly.		✓			✓		✓			✓	
Read OSHA poster at worksite.	✓	✓	✓	✓	✓	✓	✓	✓	✓	✓	
Report all job injuries.	✓	✓	✓	✓	✓	✓	✓	✓	✓	✓	

 **Leadership and Group Dynamics**

What Makes a Leader?

Activity A

Chapter 10

Name _____

Date _____ Period _____

Think about leaders you have known at school and on the job. From your experience, which leadership skills do you feel are the most important? Rate the following leadership skills and qualities in order of importance to you from 1 (most important) to 15 (least important). Then work with a small group of classmates to determine the top five choices of your group. Report your group's findings to the class. (Ratings are student response.)

_____ Has the ability to motivate team members to support a vision and achieve goals.

_____ Assumes responsibility for the duties of the office or position.

_____ Always shows confidence.

_____ Keeps the team focused.

_____ Analyzes situations clearly and takes decisive action when needed.

_____ Takes risks and explores new ways of achieving goals.

_____ Encourages team spirit and cooperation among members.

_____ Listens to others and responds to their views.

_____ Delegates assignments fairly.

_____ Recognizes the accomplishments of others.

_____ Welcomes new ideas.

_____ Sets a good example for members.

_____ Works for group, not personal, success.

_____ Does a fair share of work.

_____ Stays up-to-date on important issues.

What other skills or abilities do you feel a leader should possess?

(Answers may vary.) gives clear directions; demonstrates consistency in all actions; ensures appropriate training

is provided _____

_____

_____

_____

_____

Evaluating Leaders

Activity B

Chapter 10

Name_____

Date_____Period_____

Read the following list of leadership qualities. If the leadership quality is a positive quality, write *P* in the blank. Write *N* in the blank if the leadership quality is negative. Then in the chart below, name local or national leaders that impress you and explain why.   (Chart answers are student response.)

____P____ 1. Sets goals that have been expressed by the group.

____P____ 2. Is able to delegate responsibility.

____N____ 3. Appoints only friends to committees.

____N____ 4. Does not listen to the opinions of others.

____P____ 5. Gives credit to others for the work they do.

____P____ 6. Challenges and encourages others to action.

____P____ 7. Works for group success.

____N____ 8. Works only for personal success.

____P____ 9. Assumes the responsibility for the duties of the office.

____P____ 10. Analyzes situations clearly and will take decisive action when needed.

____P____ 11. Shows confidence in ability to lead a group.

____P____ 12. Is enthusiastic.

____N____ 13. Cannot motivate the group.

____P____ 14. Has a vision that is important to the organization.

____N____ 15. Gets others to do all the work.

Impressive Leaders	
Name of Leader:	**Key Quality or Ability**

Leadership and Group Dynamics

Activity C

Chapter 10

Name_____

Date_____ Period_____

Read the case studies below to determine the types of leadership and group dynamics illustrated in each. Explain the reason for your decisions by answering the questions that follow.

Case 1. At a staff meeting, Robin mentioned that a social activity planned for Friday interfered with the religious holiday of some employees. It was brought to her attention right before the meeting. Robin has always tried to be fair and courteous to coworkers from other cultures. Consequently, all her coworkers listen to her and value her comments. Robin asked for discussion on rescheduling the event and her coworkers agreed. They felt everyone would benefit if the social event were held on an alternative date.

What type of leadership did Robin demonstrate? Explain. Earned authority. Robin is viewed as a knowledgeable and respected member of the department, and others value her opinion.

_____

_____

_____

What group dynamics were evident at the meeting? The group dynamics evident include: a spirit of cooperation, positive interaction, and understanding and respect for diversity in the workplace.

_____

_____

_____

Case 2. There was an opening posted for a team leader on the evening shift at the music store where Tyrone and Doug work. Both Tyrone and Doug applied for the position. The new store manager had not worked with the staff very long. He selected Tyrone as team leader because Tyrone had worked there longer. As the new team leader, Tyrone immediately made changes in work schedules that gave his best friend, Cliff, Friday and Saturday evenings off. Tyrone also assigned Doug the undesirable task of restocking store items. Team members were unhappy that weekend shifts and job tasks were no longer rotated.

What type of leadership did Tyrone demonstrate? Explain. Position authority. Tyrone was officially appointed team leader by the store manager, but has not gained the respect of team members so does not possess earned authority.

_____

_____

What group dynamics are likely to occur because of the new team leader's decisions? The group dynamics likely to occur include: group conflict and arguing over unfair schedules and task assignments leading to low morale, resistance to follow orders, possible resignations, and/or complaints to the store manager. (Customers may also receive less than satisfactory treatment as a result of disgruntled or too few store employees.)

_____

Career and Technical Student Organizations

Activity D

Chapter 10

Name_____

Date_____Period_____

Working with two or three classmates, research career and technical student organizations (CTSOs). Use the letter clues to determine formal names. You may want to interview members of the organization at your school or access the Web sites noted in the chapter to gather facts. Use the information to complete the chart below. If you have a CTSO at your school that is not listed, add it to the chart.

CTSO Clues	Formal Name	Target Membership	Mission or Goal	At your school?
BPA	Business Professionals of America	middle school, high school, college	prepare students for careers in business	(Student response.)
DECA	DECA-An Association of Marketing Students	high school, college	prepare students for marketing careers	(Student response.)
FBLA	Future Business Leaders of America	middle school, high school, postsecondary	prepare students for business careers	(Student response.)
FCCLA	Family, Career and Community Leaders of America	middle school, high school	develop leadership and daily life skills	(Student response.)
FFA	National FFA Organization	12- to 21-year-olds	prepare students for agricultural science education careers	(Student response.)
HOSA	Health Occupations Students of America	high school, college	prepare students for health care careers	(Student response.)
SKILLS	SkillsUSA	high school, college	prepare students for technical, skilled, and service occupations	(Student response.)
TSA	Technology Student Association	middle school, high school	prepare students for technology-related careers	(Student response.)
Other:	(Student response.)	(Student response.)	(Student response.)	(Student response.)

Leadership Self-Evaluation

Activity E

Chapter 10

Name_____

Date_____Period_____

Evaluate your leadership skills by placing a check in the appropriate spaces. Then answer the questions that follow.
(Evaluation of leadership skills is student response.)

Leadership Skills					
How do I perform in these areas?	**Very Good**	**Good**	**Fair**	**Poor**	**Do Not Possess**
Work well with others.					
Delegate tasks fairly.					
Encourage team spirit.					
Know what is important to an organization.					
Demonstrate honesty and truthfulness.					
Use imagination and creative skills.					
Teach others new skills and knowledge.					
Help others recognize their abilities.					
Communicate clearly.					
Know and use parliamentary procedure.					
Motivate team members into action.					
Listen carefully to others.					
Use decision-making skills well.					
Set a good example.					
Keep up-to-date on new skills or ideas.					
Take responsibility for team decisions or actions.					
Work for group, not personal, success.					
Manage group conflict.					
Negotiate agreements between opposing views.					
Deal with dissatisfied "customers."					

(Continued)

Name_____

1. What other skills do you possess that will help you become a better leader? _(Sample response.)_
   knows when to intervene; treats others fairly; demonstrates resourcefulness

2. What activities and groups do you belong to that increase your skills in leadership? _(Sample response.)_
   FCCLA, band, basketball, student council

3. What new activities or groups might you join to strengthen your leadership skills? _(Sample response.)_
   drama club, football, chorus, debate team, any CTSO

4. What are some qualities of poor leadership? _(Answers may vary.)_ does not communicate effectively, does
   not treat everyone fairly, cannot motivate the group, does not give credit to others for the work they do

5. How does poor leadership affect a group's performance? _(Answers may vary.)_ Poor leadership can cause
   a group to have conflict, arguing, and jealousy leading to low morale; resistance to follow orders; possible
   resignations; and/or frequents complaints.

6. Give examples of occasions when you were a leader. _(Student response.)_

7. What frustrations have you encountered as a leader? _(Student response.)_

8. If you could give advice to a new leader at work or in a group at school, what would you say? _____
   (Sample response.) Be sure to listen to others and encourage team spirit. Help other members of the team to
   recognize their abilities.

 **Participating in Meetings**

Terms Used at Meetings

Activity A

Chapter 11

Name _____

Date _____ Period _____

The following terms are often used in meetings. Match each term with its description by writing the correct letter in the blank.

_____A_____ 1. To end a meeting.

_____B_____ 2. A list of things to be done and discussed at a meeting.

_____C_____ 3. To change the wording of a motion that has been made.

_____F_____ 4. The presiding officer at a meeting, such as the president or chairperson.

_____G_____ 5. To speak for or against a motion.

_____H_____ 6. At least one more than half of the members present at the meeting.

_____I_____ 7. A written record of the business covered at a meeting.

_____E_____ 8. The rules and regulations that govern the organization.

_____L_____ 9. An orderly way of conducting a business meeting that helps groups conduct meetings in an efficient and fair manner.

_____J_____ 10. A recommendation by a member that certain action is taken by the group.

_____M_____ 11. The number of members who must be present to legally conduct business at a meeting.

_____N_____ 12. The approval of a motion by another member.

_____P_____ 13. To delay making a decision on a motion.

_____Q_____ 14. The right to speak in a meeting without interruption from others.

_____D_____ 15. The formal term for *yes*.

_____O_____ 16. Permanent committees of the group.

A. adjourn
B. agenda
C. amend the motion
D. aye
E. bylaws
F. chair
G. debate
H. majority
I. minutes
J. motion
K. nay
L. parliamentary procedure
M. quorum
N. second the motion
O. standing committees
P. table the motion
Q. the floor

Order of Business

Activity B   Name _____

Chapter 11   Date _____ Period _____

Unscramble the order of business for a meeting by numbering the following parts of a meeting according to the parliamentary procedure discussed in the text. Then answer the questions below.

_____5_____   Marsha, chairperson of the banquet committee, gives her report.

_____6_____   A motion to hold a bake sale, which was tabled from the last meeting, is discussed.

_____9_____   Jim announces that the paper drive will continue for another week and group members should bring papers in on Friday.

_____1_____   Jane, the president, calls the meeting to order.

_____8_____   Maria, the program chairperson, introduces the guest speaker.

_____10_____   After a motion and a second motion, Jane declares the meeting adjourned.

_____2_____   Bill, the secretary, reads the minutes of the previous meeting.

_____7_____   An idea for a group picnic is brought up.

_____3_____   Jerry, the treasurer, gives his report.

_____4_____   Juan, chairperson of the membership committee, gives his report.

What is the purpose of using parliamentary procedure to conduct a meeting?

Parliamentary procedure helps groups conduct meetings in an efficient and fair manner. _____

_____

_____

_____

_____

_____

_____

_____

What items are on a typical meeting agenda from your group?

(Sample response.) reading the minutes of the previous meeting, officer's reports, standing committee reports,

special committee reports, unfinished and new business, special speakers or presentations, announcements

_____

_____

_____

_____

_____

_____

_____

Organization Constitutions and Bylaws

Activity C

Chapter 11

Name_____

Date _____ Period_____

Obtain and read a copy of the constitution and bylaws of a school organization you belong to or might like to join. Then answer the following questions and report your findings to the class.

1. What is the purpose of the organization? (Sample response.) The purpose of the organization is to
   prepare high school and college students for careers in trade, technical, and skilled service occupations,
   including health occupations.

2. What is the order of business that is followed by this organization? (Sample response.) call to order,
   reading and approving minutes, reports of officers, standing committee reports, special committee reports,
   unfinished business, new business, the program, announcements, adjournment

3. Does this organization base its meetings on parliamentary procedure? Explain. (Sample response.) Yes.
   Parliamentary procedures at all meetings are governed by *Robert's Rules of Order.*

(Continued)

Name_____

4. According to the constitution and bylaws, what is a quorum? (Sample response.) two-thirds of total chapter membership

_____

_____

5. What are the organization's standing committees? (Sample response.) nominating committee, finance committee

_____

_____

_____

_____

_____

6. How are officers nominated and elected? (Sample response.) Officers are nominated by a nominating committee and elected by secret ballot.

_____

_____

_____

_____

_____

_____

7. How are committee chairpersons selected? (Sample response.) Committee chairpersons are appointed by the president.

_____

_____

_____

8. How are motions handled? (Sample response.) A presenter of a motion is acknowledged by the president and then the motion must be seconded. Once the motion is seconded, a vote is taken of all members present.

_____

_____

_____

_____

Conducting a Meeting

Activity D

Chapter 11

Name_____

Date_____ Period_____

Work in small groups to participate in a class-wide mock meeting that uses the rules of parliamentary procedure. With two or three classmates, prepare one of the orders of business listed below. (Your teacher may make group assignments.) Then, at the appropriate time, present your group's portion of the meeting. After the meeting, answer the questions that follow.

Call to Order

Select a person to act as president of the group. Then, as a group, prepare an agenda following *Robert's Rules of Order* and discuss what the president will do during the meeting. The president will conduct the meeting following the agenda your group prepares.

Reading and Approving of Minutes

Select a person to act as secretary. As a group, prepare minutes from your last meeting, which the secretary will read during the mock meeting. Also discuss what the secretary will do during the meeting. Select another member of the group to take minutes of the current meeting.

Reports of Officers

Select a person to act as treasurer. Prepare a treasurer's report using the following information: beginning balance—$120; money collected from dues—$345; refreshments for the last meeting—$30; state dues paid—$300. Then discuss what the treasurer will do during the meeting.

Standing Committee Reports

Select a chairperson for this committee. Prepare a report on refreshments for the next meeting. What refreshments will you have? How much money will be needed? Who will purchase the refreshments? Who will set up the refreshments and clean up after the meeting? How much money must each member contribute? When is the money due?

Special Committee

Select a chairperson for this committee. Prepare a report on all aspects of painting a poster for homecoming. Who will secure a site for hanging the poster? What materials will you need? Who will get the materials? What is the theme? When will you paint the poster? Who will clean up?

Unfinished Business

Select a chairperson for this committee. The chairperson will announce that a motion to have a fund-raiser was tabled at the last meeting. Discuss the advantages or disadvantages of selling candy in school.

New Business, Announcements, and Adjournment

Select a chairperson for this committee. The chairperson will announce that a date for the next meeting should be set. You will also make an announcement about the district elections, which will be held on October 1 at the Town City Center on Main Street. Be sure to discuss the attire for the day, which is business dress. This group should also move for adjournment at the appropriate time.

1. Was a quorum present? (Student response.) _____

2. What number of people represented a quorum? (Student response.) _____

3. Did the president prepare and follow an agenda based on *Robert's Rules of Order*? (Student response.) _____

4. Did the president ask for corrections or additions to the minutes? (Student response.) _____

(Continued)

Name_____

5. Was the treasurer's report accurate? _(Student response.)_____

6. Did the standing committee include all necessary information in its report? _(Student response.)_____

7. Did the special committee include all necessary information in its report? _(Student response.)_____

8. Did the committee for unfinished business lead the discussion on the candy sale? _(Student response.)_

9. Did the committee for new business achieve its purpose? _(Student response.)_____

10. Did the announcement contain complete information? _(Student response.)_____

11. Was the motion to adjourn stated properly? _(Student response.)_____

12. What did you learn from the mock meeting that can be applied to real meetings you attend in the future?

_(Student response.)_____

_____

_____

_____

_____

_____

_____

_____

_____

_____

_____

_____

_____

_____

_____

_____

_____

_____

_____

_____

_____

_____

Learning About Yourself

How I See Myself

Activity A

Chapter 12

Name _____

Date _____ Period _____

Your self-concept is the mental image you have of yourself. Complete the following chart with information about yourself. Then answer the questions on the next page. Your answers to these questions will help you make future career decisions.   (Chart answers are student response.)

At school:	What I Do Well	What I Enjoy Doing	What I Also Want to Do
At school:			
At work:			
At home indoors:			
At home outdoors:			
With friends:			

(Continued)

Name_____
(Answers are student response.)

List three adjectives your coworkers or classmates use to describe you.

_____

_____

_____

List three adjectives your teachers or supervisor use to describe you.

_____

_____

_____

How would you describe yourself?

_____

_____

_____

What are the principles, beliefs, and values you consider important?

_____

_____

Think about how your lifestyle goals will change as you complete high school and mature into adulthood. What realistic goals do you have for when you are twenty-five, forty, and sixty-five?

_____

_____

_____

_____

_____

Abilities are skills that you possess or tasks that you can do. Check the top five strongest abilities you currently possess. Circle any skills you would like to further develop. Add any skills you possess that are not listed.

_____ Technical		_____ Public speaking	
_____ Good with people		_____ Flexible	
_____ Writing		_____ Responsible	
_____ Mathematical		_____ Quick learner	
_____ Physical		_____ Good listener	
_____ Reading		_____ Creative	
_____ Multilingual		_____ Communication	
_____ Problem solver		_____ Motivator	
_____ Organization		_____ Business sense	
_____ Computer software		_____ Self-disciplined	
_____ Positive attitude			

Other skills:_____

_____

Identifying Personal Interests

Activity B

Chapter 12

Name_____

Date _____ Period _____

Your personal interests, abilities, and aptitudes can help you identify careers that will interest you. Look at each statement below and place a check in the column that indicates your level of interest. Then answer the questions that follow. (There are no right or wrong answers.)   (Chart answers are student response.)

	Very Much	Somewhat	No Opinion	Probably Not	No
1. I like working with people.					
2. I prefer to work alone.					
3. I like to work with animals.					
4. I like to work with plants.					
5. I prefer to work outdoors.					
6. I prefer to work indoors.					
7. I would like to explore and invent.					
8. I like science-related activities.					
9. I like creating music or playing an instrument.					
10. I want to use my design skills and ideas.					
11. I like to act.					
12. I like working with tools and machines.					
13. I like working with facts and figures.					
14. I want to sing or dance professionally.					
15. I like working with children.					
16. I like working with elderly people.					
17. I like to care for sick people.					
18. I like to paint or create artwork.					
19. I enjoy creative or report writing.					
20. I like long-range planning.					
21. I want to use my computer skills.					
22. I like selling and persuading others.					
23. I like to coach or teach others.					
24. I enjoy speaking in front of groups.					
25. I like to investigate clues and solve problems.					

(Continued)

Name_____

(Answers are student response.)

Choose your top five interests from the chart and list them here.

1. _____

2. _____

3. _____

4. _____

5. _____

Based on your top five interests, describe your idea of an ideal career.

_____

_____

_____

_____

_____

What aptitudes would an individual need for this career? Circle those you possess.

_____

_____

_____

_____

_____

_____

_____

_____

What abilities do you need to perform well in this career?

_____

_____

_____

_____

_____

_____

_____

_____

_____

Identifying Your Personality Traits

Activity C
Chapter 12

Name_____

Date_____ Period_____

Working in small groups, prepare a general list of personality traits in the space provided. Then work alone to consider your own personality traits and list them in the space below. (You may repeat personality traits from the general list.)

General Personality Traits
(Answers may vary.)

Adaptable	Dedicated	Open-minded
Artistic	Detail-oriented	Patient
Calm	Driven	Protective
Compassionate	Enterprising	Questioning
Competitive	Enthusiastic	Responsible
Courageous	Helpful	Self-reliant
Courteous	Honest	Social
Decisive	Loyal	Stable

My Personality Traits
(Student response.)

Traits I Possess

Traits I Want to Develop

Traits I Need for Career Success

Matching Traits and Abilities to Jobs

Activity D

Chapter 12

Name_____

Date_____Period_____

Work with three or four classmates to complete the following team assignment. Assume you are employees at a computer software company. Your team has been asked to analyze personality traits, abilities, and skills needed for the various positions available in your company. The information you provide will be used to develop job descriptions. Research the available jobs listed below. Then complete the information needed under each category.   (Sample responses are shown.)

Job	Personality Traits Needed	Abilities Needed	Skills/Aptitudes Needed
Computer programmer:	Dependable	Deductive reasoning	Programming
	Independent	Oral comprehension	Critical thinking
	Detail-oriented	Written expression	Active listening
	Flexible	Problem sensitivity	Technology design
Customer service representative:	Cooperative	Deductive reasoning	Service orientation
	Detail-oriented	Speech clarity	Critical thinking
	Calm	Information ordering	Time management
	Adaptable	Problem sensitivity	Active listening
Word processor:	Independent	Finger dexterity	Decision-making
	Cooperative	Category flexibility	Critical thinking
	Dependable	Written comprehension	Active listening
	Detail-oriented	Perceptual speed	Learning strategies
Accountant:	Independent	Mathematical reasoning	Mathematics
	Detail-oriented	Deductive reasoning	Systems analysis
	Honest	Problem sensitivity	Critical thinking
	Logical	Informational ordering	Active learning
Sales manager:	Persistent	Oral expression	Persuasion
	Flexible	Problem sensitivity	Monitoring
	Cooperative	Originality	Service orientation
	Independent	Inductive reasoning	Social perceptiveness

Values, Goals, Standards, and Resources

Activity E

Chapter 12

Name_____

Date_____Period_____

Relate your values, goals, standards, and resources to your future career by following the directions below.

1. List your top five values in order of priority. (There are no right or wrong answers.) (Student response.)

   _____ _____

   _____ _____

   _____ _____

   _____ _____

   _____ _____

2. List your career goals—three short-term goals and one long-term goal. (Student response.)

   Short-term goals:

   _____

   _____

   _____

   Long-term goal:

   _____

3. Describe how your career goals and values are related. (Student response.)

   _____

   _____

4. Explain whether you set high or low standards for yourself. (Student response.)

   _____

   _____

5. Explain how your standards are related to your values and goals. (Student response.)

   _____

   _____

6. List your human resources and explain how they can help in attaining your career goals. _____
   (Student response.)

   _____

   _____

7. List your nonhuman resources and explain how they can help in attaining your career goals._____
   (Student response.)

   _____

A Learning Review

Activity F   Name _____

Chapter 12   Date _____ Period _____

Match the following terms to the correct definition. Then answer the questions below.

____K____   1. All the goods and services a person considers essential for living.

____H____   2. Something you want to achieve in a short period of time.

____O____   3. Principles and beliefs you feel are important.

____M____   4. Material things you have to achieve goals.

____B____   5. The process of taking stock of your interests, aptitudes, and abilities.

____I____   6. Something you want to achieve in the months and years to come.

____J____   7. Accepted levels of achievement.

____N____   8. Set of moral principles or values that guide a person's conduct.

____L____   9. Your skills, knowledge, and experience.

____F____   10. Doing something the same way every time.

____D____   11. What you want from your life.

____A____   12. The mental image you have of yourself.

____C____   13. A person's natural physical and mental talents for learning.

____E____   14. Physical and mental powers to perform a task or skill well.

____G____   15. How a person thinks, feels, and interacts with others.

A. self-concept
B. self-assessment
C. aptitude
D. lifestyle goals
E. ability
F. habit
G. personality
H. short-term goal
I. long-term goal
J. standards
K. standard of living
L. human resources
M. nonhuman resources
N. ethics
O. values

16. What is an example of unethical behavior? _(Answers may vary.) a person tries to take credit for someone_ _else's work; an employee calls in when he or she is not sick_ _____

_____

17. What are two examples of human resources helpful in attaining career goals? _(Answers may vary.)_ _skills, knowledge, experience, determination, motivation, imagination_ _____

_____

18. What methods are available for individuals to find out the aptitudes they possess? _personal work_ _experience, testing, GATB_ _____

_____

13 Learning About Careers

Career Clues and Clusters

Activity A

Chapter 13

Name_____

Date_____Period_____

Read about the career clusters in Chapter 13. Then read the career clues below. Next to each career clue, identify the appropriate career cluster and career pathway.   (See text pages 252–283 for pathways.)

Career Clue:

Career Cluster:

1. I am a receptionist for a large corporation. — business, management, and administration

2. I grow apples in a large orchard. — agriculture, food, and natural resources

3. I am a sheet-metal worker. — architecture and construction

4. I am an X-ray technician at a medical center. — health science

5. I care for infants in a child care center. — human services

6. I design sets for the local theater. — arts, audio/visual technology, and communication

7. I build houses. — architecture and construction

8. I am a barber. — human services

9. I manage a resort hotel. — hospitality and tourism

10. I landscape buildings downtown. — agriculture, food, and natural resources

11. I am a help-desk technician. — information technology

12. I drive a taxi. — transportation, distribution, and logistics

13. I am a welder at a factory. — manufacturing

14. I am a paralegal. — law, public safety, corrections, and security

15. I help people make financial plans. — finance

16. I research the plant and animal life of oceans. — science, technology, engineering, and mathematics

17. I am a sales representative for a food company. — marketing, sales, and service

18. I am an air traffic controller at the airport. — transportation, distribution, and logistics

19. I am a school psychologist. — education and training

20. I am an economic development coordinator. — government and public administration

21. I am a firefighter. — law, public safety, corrections, and security

22. I assist hospital patients with dietary needs. — agriculture, food, and natural resources; health science

23. I am a data analyst. — information technology

24. I enter financial data into a computer. — finance

25. I am a nanny. — education and training; human services

Occupation Interview

Activity B   **Name**_____

Chapter 13   **Date**_____**Period**_____

Choose a nontraditional occupation that appeals to you. Contact and interview a person employed in this occupation. Find out the answers to the following questions. Prepare at least two questions of your own. Discuss your interview experience in class. (Answers are student response.)

Occupation:

1. How long have you worked in this occupation? _____

2. How and why did you decide on this occupation?_____

    _____

    _____

3. How and where did you obtain your training and education for this occupation? _____

    _____

    _____

4. Do you enjoy your occupation? _____

5. Would you go into this line of work again? Explain. _____

    _____

6. What advice would you give to someone considering this occupation? _____

    _____

    _____

7. Is a license or certificate required by law to work in your occupation? If so, please describe the

    procedure to obtain it. _____

    _____

8. What do you see as the future trends for this occupation? _____

    _____

    _____

9. Write two additional questions below. Then write the responses given. _____

    Question: _____

    Response:_____

    _____

    Question: _____

    Response:_____

    _____

Occupational Interests

Activity C   Name _____

Chapter 13   Date _____ Period _____

For each of the 16 career clusters listed here, name and describe two occupations. Then indicate the level of education each occupation requires. Finally, place a check mark next to each occupation that interests you. (The occupations you list do not have to be those listed in the text.)   (Sample responses are shown.)

Career Cluster	Description	Education Required
Agriculture, food, and natural resources		
1. nutritionist	plans food programs	bachelor's degree
2. welder	joins metal parts	high school/training
Architecture and construction		
1. interior designer	decorates interior spaces	bachelor's degree
2. roofer	repairs/installs roofs	high school/training
Arts, audiovisual (A/V) technology, and communications		
1. curator	preserves objects	master's degree
2. reporter	investigates stories	bachelor's degree
Business, management, and administration		
1. billing clerk	prepares bills	high school/training
2. paralegal	assists lawyers	associate's degree
Education and training		
1. audiologist	treats hearing problems	master's degree
2. child care worker	supervises children	high school
Finance		
1. loan officer	guides loan applicants	bachelor's degree
2. tax examiner	reviews tax returns	bachelor's degree
Government and public administration		
1. legislator	develops laws	elected official
2. revenue agent	audits tax returns	bachelor's degree
Health science		
1. speech/language pathologist	treats speech disorders	master's degree
2. transcriptionist	transcribes reports	associate's degree
Hospitality and tourism		
1. chef	prepares food	high school/training
2. event planner	coordinates events	bachelor's degree

(Continued)

Name_____

Human services

1. career counselor _____ provides career counseling — master's degree

2. hairstylist _____ styles hair — high school/training

Information technology

1. computer support specialist _____ gives technical support — high school/training

2. computer systems administrator _____ designs computer systems — bachelor's degree

Law, public safety, corrections, and security

1. correctional officer _____ maintains jail security — high school/training

2. firefighter _____ fights fires — high school/training

Manufacturing

1. boilermaker _____ makes boilers — apprenticeship

2. environmental engineer _____ solves environmental issues — bachelor's degree

Marketing, sales, and service

1. merchandise buyer _____ purchases merchandise — bachelor's degree

2. sales associate _____ sells merchandise — high school

Science, technology, engineering, and mathematics

1. astronomer _____ conducts research — doctoral degree

2. nuclear engineer _____ researches nuclear energy — bachelor's degree

Transportation, distribution, and logistics

1. flight attendant _____ ensures flight comfort — high school/training

2. travel agent _____ makes travel arrangements — high school/training

Review your occupation choices. Select five that most interest you and list them below. Research your choices using the *Occupational Outlook Handbook* Web site (www.bls.gov/oco/). Describe two aspects of each occupation you find appealing. (Occupation choices are student response.)

1. _____

2. _____

3. _____

4. _____

5. _____

_____

_____

_____

_____

Researching Careers

Library Research

Activity A	Name_____
Chapter 14	Date_____ Period_____

Choose two occupations and visit the library to research them. Using at least three sources of information in the library, answer the following questions.   (Sample responses are shown.)

Occupation 1: _Interior Designer_

Occupation 2: _Physical Therapist_

1. What library sources of occupational information were used? _Occupational Outlook Quarterly,_
   Occupational Outlook Handbook, Career Guide to Industries

2. How are the occupations described?

   Occupation 1: _Commonly uses computer-aided design (CAD) to create designs for interior spaces._
   Generally focuses on decorating and architectural detail. Frequently works with architects, electricians, and
   building contractors. Often specializes in one area of expertise.

   Occupation 2: _Develops programs and provides treatment to individuals suffering from injuries or_
   disease. Treatments often include exercises to improve mobility, decrease pain, and limit permanent
   physical disabilities.

3. What is the wage or salary range?

   Occupation 1: _Salaries vary widely but individuals working in larger design and architectural firms_
   usually have a higher salary.

   Occupation 2: _Salaries vary widely based on location and level of expertise._

4. What are the future job prospects?

   Occupation 1: _Competition for positions will be difficult due to a large interest in the field._

   Occupation 2: _Employment is anticipated to grow much faster than average and job prospects will be_
   good.

Using the Internet

Activity B   Name _____

Chapter 14   Date _____ Period _____

Using the Internet, research the occupations chosen in Activity A. Use at least three Web sites to answer the following questions. (Sample responses are shown.)

Occupation 1: _Interior Designer_

Occupation 2: _Physical Therapist_

1. What Web sites did you visit? _Occupational Outlook Handbook (www.bls.gov/oco); Career Voyages_ _(www.careervoyages.gov/); CareerOneStop (www.careeronestop.org)_

2. What other career exploration sites did you research? _America's Career InfoNet (www.careerinfonet.org);_ _O*Net™ online (www.online.onetcenter.org)_

3. What job outlook and future trends exist for each?

   Occupation 1: _Ergonomic, elder, and environmental areas of design are expected to be in demand in the_ _future. If the economy grows, jobs may be in higher demand. However, if decreases in spending occur, it_ _will have a very negative effect on employment._

   Occupation 2: _Increase in the elderly population, future medical developments, and interest in health_ _promotion should increase the demand for physical therapy services. Job outlook is good due to the_ _availability of more employment opportunities than candidates._

4. What training or education is needed?

   Occupation 1: _bachelor's degree, apprenticeship program, licensing exam, continuing education to_ _maintain licensure_

   Occupation 2: _master's degree from an accredited physical therapist education program (a doctoral degree_ _may become the future entry-level requirement), state license with passing scores on state and national_ _exams, continuing education to maintain licensure_

Your Guidance Counselor

Activity C

Chapter 14

Name _____

Date _____ Period _____

Visit your guidance counselor. (If you are in the process of trying to determine a career interest, your counselor can help you to explore your options.) Research the occupations chosen in Activities A and B by discussing them with your counselor. Find answers to the following questions about the occupations you have chosen. (Sample responses are shown.)

Occupation 1: Interior Designer _____

Occupation 2: Physical Therapist _____

1. What are the entry requirements for the job?

   Occupation 1: Entry-level positions require a bachelor's degree, an apprenticeship program or equivalent work experience, and a license.

   _____

   Occupation 2: Entry-level positions currently require a master's degree from an accredited physical therapist education program (a doctoral degree may become the future entry-level requirement) and a state license.

2. What education or training is needed?

   Occupation 1: bachelor's degree, 1- to 3-year apprenticeship, licensing exam, continuing education to maintain licensure

   _____

   Occupation 2: master's degree from an accredited program, a state license with passing scores on state and national exams, continuing education to maintain licensure

   _____

3. What schools, colleges, training programs, or registered apprenticeships offer the education you need?

   Occupation 1: For a list of college programs, contact the National Association of Schools of Art and Design.

   _____

   _____

   Occupation 2: For a list of accredited physical therapist education programs, contact the American Physical Therapy Association.

   _____

   _____

4. Who is your guidance counselor?

   (name) _____

Talking with Workers

Activity D   **Name**_____

Chapter 14   **Date**_____**Period**_____

Consult workers in an informal interview to find out the following information about the occupations you have researched in Activities A, B, and C. (Conduct an informal interview with one person employed in Occupation 1 and one person employed in Occupation 2.)   (Interviews are student response.)

Occupation 1: _____ Person contacted: _____

Occupation 2: _____ Person contacted: _____

1. Describe the duties, hours, working conditions, salary range, fringe benefits, etc.

   Occupation 1: _____

   _____

   _____

   Occupation 2: _____

   _____

   _____

2. What are the advantages and opportunities for advancement?

   Occupation 1: _____

   _____

   Occupation 2: _____

   _____

3. What are the drawbacks of the job?

   Occupation 1: _____

   _____

   Occupation 2: _____

   _____

4. What advice would you give to someone considering a job in this field?

   Occupation 1: _____

   _____

   Occupation 2: _____

   _____

   _____

   _____

Sources for Career Research

Activity E

Chapter 14

Name_____

Date_____Period_____

Many sources of information are available to help you research careers. A few sources of career information with certain letters missing are given below. Supply the missing letters. Then complete each statement in the space provided.

1. Informal interviews with **w** o **r k** e **r** s who are in jobs that interest you can result in _insight into careers, future job contacts, and practice interviewing_

2. Your school and local **l** i **b** r a **r** i e **s** are both important sources of career information because_they provide a wide variety of materials_

3. The O **c c** u **p** a **t** i o **n** a **l** O u **t** l o **o k** H a **n** d **b** o **o k** is an excellent career information guide because _it describes the training and education needed for various occupations, expected earnings, working conditions, and future job prospects_

4. The **C** a **r** e **e** r G u **i** d e **t o** I **n** d **u s t** r i **e s** can be used as a companion with the *Occupational Outlook Handbook*. It gives individuals more information on _expected earnings, working conditions, future job prospects, and links to information about each state's job market_

5. Using the Internet for career **r** e **s** e **a** r **c** h gives you access to _a wealth of information at your fingertips_

6. **D** o **l** e **t** a.gov is a Web site that has online tools for_examining your interests and personality to help identify suitable careers_

7. A guidance **c** o **u n** s e **l** o **r** can help you explore career options by providing_up-to-date information about specific careers and relating your abilities and goals to various career options_

8. School **c** a **r** e **e** r **d** a **y** s let students talk to representatives of _various occupations, professions, and schools_

Evaluating Careers

Activity F

Chapter 14

Name_____

Date_____Period_____

Evaluate the two occupations you researched in Activities A, B, C, and D by answering the questions below. When you have completed your analysis, exchange your evaluations with a classmate and review each other's work.   (Answers are student response.)

Occupation 1: _____

Occupation 2: _____

1. What are the general working hours?

   Occupation 1: _____

   Occupation 2: _____

2. What is the salary range?

   Occupation 1: _____

   Occupation 2: _____

3. How well does the occupation fit your personal lifestyle and goals?

   Occupation 1: _____

   _____

   _____

   Occupation 2: _____

   _____

   _____

4. How well does the occupation match your interests, aptitudes, and abilities?

   Occupation 1: _____

   _____

   _____

   Occupation 2: _____

   _____

   _____

5. Based upon your research results, how would you evaluate your ability to succeed in the occupation?

   Occupation 1: _____

   _____

   _____

   Occupation 2: _____

   _____

   _____

Making Career Decisions

Examining Decisions

Activity A	Name _____
Chapter 15	Date _____ Period _____

In your own words, define the terms below. Then read the questions in the chart and determine what type of decision is needed. Write either *major* or *routine* in the middle column and explain your choice.

Definition of *major decision*: _Tough choices requiring careful thought because they affect a person's career and personal life._

Definition of *routine decision*: _Choices that most people make automatically about everyday matters, such as what to eat and wear._

Question	Type of Decision	Explanation
1. Should I get married?	major	(Sample response.) This is a decision that can affect a person's life.
2. Which snack should I eat?	routine	(Sample response.) This is a choice about an everyday matter and is usually made automatically.
3. What outfit will I wear today?	routine	(Sample response.) This is a choice about an everyday matter and is usually made automatically.
4. Should I go to college?	major	(Sample response.) This is a decision that can affect a person's life.
5. Which career is best for me?	major	(Sample response.) This is a decision that can affect a person's life.
6. When should I go shopping?	routine	(Sample response.) This is a choice about an everyday matter and is usually made automatically.

The Decision-Making Process

Activity B

Chapter 15

Name_____

Date_____Period_____

Refer to the two occupations you researched in Chapter 14 for Activities A, B, C, D, and F. Using the decision-making steps below, decide which of the occupations would suit you best.
(Answers are student response.)

1. Define the problem (or question): _____

   _____

   _____

2. Establish your goals: _____

   _____

   _____

3. Identify your resources: _____

   _____

   _____

4. Consider the alternatives: _____

   _____

   _____

5. Make a decision:_____

   _____

   _____

6. Implement the decision (or explain how you would do this in the future): _____

   _____

   _____

7. Evaluate the results of your occupational decision. (What are some future clues that you made the right choice?): _____

   _____

   _____

   _____

   _____

   _____

   _____

   _____

Preparing a Career Plan

Activity C

Chapter 15

Name_____

Date_____Period_____

Prepare a career plan below for the career decision you made in Activity B. You may refer to the career plan shown in 15-5 in the text. (Sample responses are shown.)

Career plan for Physical Therapist _____

	Extracurricular and Volunteer Activities	**Work Experience**	**Education and Training**
During junior high school	Participate in activities promoting fitness and health.	Help take care of a child with physical disabilities.	For optional or extra-credit work, select topics and do projects pertaining to social sciences or math.
During high school	Assist the school athletic trainer.	Work part-time at a nursing home or group home for people with physical disabilities.	Take a college preparatory program emphasizing biology, chemistry, and physics.
During college	Attend seminars and workshops on physical disabilities and medical developments.	Work part-time at a hospital or clinic.	Take a doctoral degree program at an accredited physical therapist education program.
After college	Keep up-to-date on medical developments and volunteer expertise as needed.	Work full-time as a physical therapist for the local hospital.	Pass the state and national licensing exam. Continue education by participating in courses and workshops.

Preparing a Career Ladder

Activity D

Chapter 15

Name_____

Date_____Period_____

Prepare a career ladder for the career decision you made in Activity B. Use the *Occupational Outlook Handbook* and the Internet for references. (Sample responses are shown.)

Career ladder for Physical Therapist_____

Advanced degree

- Physical therapist
- Teacher in an academic institution
- Consultant/private practice

Bachelor's degree

- Physical therapy assistant, hospital
- Physical therapy assistant, nursing home
- Physical therapy assistant, rehabilitation center

Advanced training/ associates degree

- Adult day care program aide
- Rehabilitation aide

High school diploma

- Physical therapy aide
- Nursing aide

Part-time jobs during high school

- Home health aide
- Personal care aide

It's Your Decision

Activity E

Chapter 15

Name_____

Date_____ Period_____

Besides career decisions, you must also make important decisions relating to other areas of your life. The decision-making process can help you make those decisions. Think of an important decision you must make relating to your personal life, your job, or a consumer purchase. Then, apply the decision-making process described in the text. (Answers are student response.)

1. Identify the problem:_____

_____

_____

2. List your goals:_____

_____

_____

3. Identify and list your resources: _____

_____

_____

4. Consider the alternatives. List the pros and cons of each choice.

Choice #1:

Pros:_____

_____
_____
_____
_____
_____

Cons: _____

_____
_____
_____
_____
_____

Choice #2:

Pros:_____

_____
_____
_____
_____

Cons: _____

_____
_____
_____
_____

(Continued)

Name_____

(Answers are student response.)

5. Make the decision: _____

_____

_____

_____

_____

6. Implement the decision. List the steps you will follow to carry out your decision:

A. _____

_____

B. _____

_____

C. _____

_____

D. _____

_____

7. Evaluate the results of your decision: _____

_____

_____

_____

_____

_____

_____

_____

8. What have you learned from applying the decision-making process to an important decision? _____

_____

_____

_____

_____

_____

_____

_____

_____

16 Applying for Jobs

Checking Want Ads

Activity A

Chapter 16

Name_____

Date_____ Period_____

Clip two newspaper advertisements for jobs that interest you and mount them in the space below. For each, list the address, fax number, or e-mail to which résumés should be sent. If the information is given, also list the employers' names, the names of the people to contact, phone numbers, and Web sites.
(Want ads information is student response.)

Want Ad 1	Want Ad 2

Address for résumé: _____   _____

_____   _____

_____   _____

_____   _____

Fax number: _____   _____

E-mail: _____   _____

Employer name: _____   _____

Contact name: _____   _____

Phone number: _____   _____

Web site: _____   _____

Your Résumé

Activity B

Chapter 16

Name_____

Date_____Period_____

In the space provided, design a résumé for yourself. Read it over carefully and ask your teacher or counselor to read it over as well. When you are happy with the résumé, enter it in a word processing document and print it on 8½×11-inch white bond paper. (Make copies of your résumé to submit to potential employers.)
(Résumé is student response. Students should follow the format provided on page 333 of the text.)

Preparing a Portfolio

Activity C

Chapter 16

Name_____

Date_____ Period_____

In the classified section of the Sunday newspaper, Jorge found an advertisement for a position as an executive assistant. Jorge phoned for an interview and plans to prepare a portfolio for it. Below is a list of items Jorge wants to put in his portfolio. Explain how each item supports Jorge's qualifications for the job described.

> Wanted: Executive assistant to a communications department manager. Exceptional organizational, writing, and computer skills.

1. Essay written in English class: _demonstrates organizational and writing skills_

2. Document prepared in a word processing program: _demonstrates computer literacy_

3. Résumé: _should always be included in a portfolio_

4. Article written for the school paper: _demonstrates organizational and writing skills_

5. Letter of application: _should always be included in a portfolio_

6. Award for first place in a state spreadsheet competition: _demonstrates computer literacy_

7. Report from a successful project completed for a club: _demonstrates organizational and writing skills as well as the ability to work as a team member_

8. Brochure designed on the computer: _demonstrates computer literacy_

List the items you would include in your portfolio for one of the jobs you selected in Activity A. Explain why you selected each one. (Student response.)

_____

_____

_____

_____

_____

_____

Telephoning an Employer

Activity D

Chapter 16

Name_____

Date_____Period_____

Mindy learned that Larry's Drugstore may have a job opening. Mindy wants to apply for the job and plans to telephone the manager for an interview. Help Mindy decide how to proceed. Read the following statements about telephoning an employer. If the statement is true, write *true* in the blank. If the statement is false, write *false* in the blank.

_____true_____ 1. Mindy's first contact with the employer may be by telephone.

_____false_____ 2. When Mindy calls about the job lead, it does not matter if she has music playing in the background.

_____true_____ 3. Mindy should make a list of questions she wants to ask before calling.

_____false_____ 4. Mindy does *not* need to be ready to briefly describe her background and qualifications for the job.

_____true_____ 5. When Mindy calls, she needs to have a pad of paper ready to take notes.

_____true_____ 6. Mindy should use a conversational voice and good manners when she calls.

_____false_____ 7. Mindy does *not* need to state the purpose of her call.

_____true_____ 8. Mindy should introduce herself when she calls.

_____false_____ 9. If during the call Mindy learns that no job opening exists, she should not waste time telling the manager she would like a job at the drugstore.

_____false_____ 10. If Mindy does not know how to get to Larry's Drugstore, she should *not* show her ignorance by asking for directions.

Fill in the boxes below to prepare yourself for your phone conversations.   (Answers are student response.)

My introduction:	**My skills and qualifications:**

My background:	**Questions about the company and interview:**

Letter of Application

Activity E

Chapter 16

Name _____

Date _____ Period _____

Choose one of the job leads you listed in Activity A. In the space below, outline a letter of application for the job. Enter the letter in a word processing document and print it on 8½×11-inch white bond paper.
(Letter of application is student response. Students should follow the format provided on page 342 of the text.)

_____

_____

_____

_____

_____

_____

_____

_____

_____

_____

_____

_____

_____

_____

_____

_____

_____

_____

_____

Checklist

The letter contains

_____ 1. the return address and date

_____ 2. a complete inside address

_____ 3. proper salutation

_____ 4. the first paragraph explaining that I am applying for a specific job and how I learned about it

_____ 5. the second paragraph giving information about my abilities to perform the particular job

_____ 6. the last paragraph asking for an interview and describing how I can be reached

_____ 7. a proper closing with my signature

Illegal Questions

Activity F

Chapter 16

Name_____

Date_____ Period_____

By law, an employer cannot ask certain questions on a job application form or in an interview. Read each question in the list and check *yes* if an employer can legally ask it. Check *no* if an employer cannot legally ask the question. Then provide an explanation to the last question.

Yes	No	
	✓	1. What is your race?
✓		2. Are you a U.S. citizen?
	✓	3. In what country were you born?
	✓	4. In what country were your parents born?
✓		5. What is your address?
	✓	6. Do you attend church?
	✓	7. Where do you go to church?
✓		8. What salary do you expect?
	✓	9. What are the ages of your children?
	✓	10. Who will care for the children while you work?
✓		11. Where did you go to college?
✓		12. Do you have dependable transportation?
	✓	13. What language do you speak at home?
	✓	14. When is your birthday?
	✓	15. What is your age?
	✓	16. Do you have any physical disabilities? (except for disabilities that prevent you from performing the job)
✓		17. Where were you previously employed?
	✓	18. To what clubs or organizations do you belong?
	✓	19. Would you attach a recent photograph to your application?
✓		20. Why did you leave your last job?

If an interviewer asked you an illegal question, how would you respond? Explain. (Student response.)

_____

_____

_____

_____

_____

_____

Filling Out a Job Application

Activity G

Chapter 16

Name _____

Date _____ Period _____

(Application is student response. Students should fill out similarly to the sample on pages 344–345 of the text.)

Application for Employment

PERSONAL INFORMATION

Date _____   Social Security Number _____

Name _____
       Last   First   Middle

Present Address _____
          Street   City   State   Zip

Permanent Address _____
          Street   City   State   Zip

Phone No. _____

If related to anyone in our employ, state name and department _____   Referred by _____

EMPLOYMENT DESIRED

Position _____   Date you can start _____   Salary desired _____

Are you employed now? _____   If so may we inquire of your present employer? _____

Ever applied to this company before? _____   Where _____   When _____

EDUCATION

	Name and Location of School	Years Completed	Subjects Studied
Grammar School			
High School			
College			
Trade, Business or Correspondence School			

Subject of special study or research work _____

(Continued)

Name_____

(Application is student response. Students should fill out similarly to the sample on pages 344–345 of the text.)

What foreign languages do you fluently speak? _____ Read? _____ Write? _____

U.S. Military or
Naval service _____ Rank _____ Present membership in
National Guard or Reserves _____

Activities other than religious
(civic, athletic, fraternal, etc.) _____

Exclude organizations the name or character of which indicates the race, creed, color or national origin of its members

FORMER EMPLOYERS List employers starting with last one first

Date Month and Year	Name and Address of Employer	Salary	Position	Reason for Leaving
From _____ To				
From _____ To				
From _____ To				
From _____ To				

REFERENCES List below at least two persons not related to you whom you have known at least one year

	Name	Address	Job Title	Years Acquainted
1				
2				
3				

PHYSICAL RECORD

Have you any defects in hearing, vision or speech that might affect your job performance?

In case of
emergency notify _____

Name	Address	Phone No.

I authorize investigation of all statements contained in this application. I understand that misrepresentation or omission of facts called for is cause for dismissal.

Date _____ Signature _____

17 Taking Preemployment Tests

Preemployment Perception Test

Activity A

Chapter 17

Name_____

Date_____Period_____

Match the item in the first column with the answer on the right that is identical. Circle the correct match. There is only one correct response for each item. You will have exactly three minutes to complete the test.

Example			
Item	**A**	**B**	**C**
Carl E. Jones	E. Carl Jones	(Carl E. Jones)	Carl F. Jones

Item	**A**	**B**	**C**
1. Linda S. Vaughan	(Linda S. Vaughan)	Linda E. Vaughan	Linda S. Vaughen
2. Manuel J. Ramiz	Maneul J. Ramiz	(Manuel J. Ramiz)	Manuel F. Ramiz
3. $867.23	($867.23)	$876.23	$867.32
4. 546-32-1145	546-23-1145	564-32-1145	(546-32-1145)
5. accessible	accesible	(accessible)	acessible
6. leisure	(leisure)	liesure	leisurre
7. tragedy	tragady	(tragedy)	tregady
8. (813) 945-3897	(813) 954-3897	(813) 945-3879	((813) 945-3897)
9. commitment	comitmment	comitment	(commitment)
10. judgment	(judgment)	judgement	judgmant
11. Galaxy Systems	Galaxey Systems	Galaxy System	(Galaxy Systems)
12. $677.20	$667.20	($677.20)	$6,777.20

Score _____

Preemployment Math Skills Testing

Activity B

Chapter 17

Name_____

Date_____ Period_____

A basic math test examines a job candidate's ability to add, subtract, multiply, divide, find percentages, and work with fractions. These skills are essential for success in many work situations. Your ability to compute the answers accurately and in a set amount of time is tested here. Check the amount of time it takes you to complete the test.

Beginning time _____

Multiplication

1. $16 \times 4 = 64$
2. $69 \times 8 = 552$
3. $36 \times 5 = 180$
4. $79 \times 2 = 158$

Addition

5. $63 + 30 + 44 + 102 = 239$
6. $44 + 57 + 60 + 32 = 193$
7. $24 + 43 + 29 + 57 = 153$
8. $37 + 63 + 3 + 16 = 119$

9. $\$84.78 + 59.50 = \$144.28$
10. $\$45.08 + 61.01 = \$106.09$
11. $\$32.12 + 12.18 = \$44.30$
12. $\$97.65 + 18.24 = \$115.89$

Subtraction

13. $55 - 32 = 23$
14. $98 - 73 = 25$
15. $67 - 19 = 48$
16. $125 - 31 = 94$

Percentages and Fractions

17. 10% of $2,800 = $280.00
18. 16¾ + ¼ = 17
19. 6½ + 10½ = 17
20. 25% of $8.00 = $2.00

End time _____

Total time _____

Score _____

Preemployment Testing

Activity C

Chapter 17

Name_____

Date_____Period_____

Indicate what types of preemployment tests might be given for the jobs that follow. Place the appropriate letters in the blanks. (Some jobs may have more than one answer.) Then answer the questions about preemployment testing. Discuss the answers in class.

A, B   1. Administrative assistant

B   2. Data processing clerk

A   3. Auto mechanic

B, C, G   4. Bank teller

D   5. Mail carrier

E   6. Armed services worker

C, D, F, G, H   7. FBI agent

H   8. Airline pilot

B, G   9. Cashier

H   10. Professional football player

A, B   11. Clerical worker

D   12. Postal clerk

A   13. Machine operator

B, H   14. Food server

C, H   15. Office manager

A. performance skill test
B. situational skill test
C. psychological test
D. civil service test
E. Armed Services Vocational Aptitude Battery tests
F. polygraph test
G. written honesty test
H. medical examination

16. What types of preemployment tests have you taken? (Student response.)

17. How can preemployment tests help you as well as your future employer? Taking a preemployment test may reinforce your interest in your chosen career. Test results may show that you are seeking a job for which you are not suited. You may find more training is needed to meet an employer's requirements, or your skills and interests are better matched to another career field.

(Continued)

18. In what ways can you prepare yourself to take a preemployment test? _Practice for skill tests. Get plenty_ _of rest the night before the test. Bring an extra pencil for written tests. Arrive at the test site early. Select a_ _seat where you can see and hear the examiner well. Ask questions about anything you do not understand._ _Follow directions exactly. Answer the easiest questions first. Have confidence in your ability._

19. How can jobs be modified for employees with the following disabilities? Explain. _____

Hearing impaired: _(Sample response.) provide interpreters fluent in sign language; provide a telephone_ _amplifier_

Visually impaired: _(Sample response.) modify job duties; use screen readers on computers_

Physically disabled: _(Sample response.) alter workspace; purchase special furniture_

20. What are the advantages and disadvantages of drug testing? _(Sample response.) advantages: safer work_ _environment, lower costs of accidents to employers, lower health costs, increased productivity; disadvan-_ _tages: right to privacy, test accuracy_

21. How has advancements in technology changed the need for testing performance skills? _____ _(Sample response.) Most jobs now require applicants to technology knowledge and abilities, and these may_ _be tested. Other skills may be tested through computers as well._

Types of Preemployment Tests

Activity D

Chapter 17

Name _____

Date _____ Period _____

Read the statements below and write the missing terms in the crossword puzzle.

						¹S	²P	E	E	D			³S	
							E						I	
			⁴P	E	R	S	O	N	A	L	I	T	Y	
							F					U		
		⁵H					O		⁶A	S	V	A	B	
	⁷P	O	L	Y	G	R	A	P	H			T		
		N				M		⁸C	I	V	I	L		
⁹C	L	E	R	I	C	A	L					O		
		S				N						N		
		T				C	¹⁰M	E	¹¹D	I	C	A	L	
		Y				E	A		R			L		
							T		U					
							H		G					

Across

1. A word processing test rates a person's _____, accuracy, and computer literacy.

4. A psychological test examines a person's _____, character, and interests.

6. The _____ is an aptitude test with a career exploration program available through the military for juniors and seniors in high school and postsecondary students.

7. Another name for a lie-detector test is a _____ test.

8. A _____ service test is an examination a person may have to take before he or she will be considered for a government job.

9. A _____ skill test is often given to applicants seeking employment as office assistants.

10. _____ examinations determine a person's physical condition for the job.

Down

2. _____ tests check your ability to operate tools and machines.

3. To test how you would actually perform on the job, you may be asked to complete a _____ test.

5. A written _____ test measures your integrity on the job.

10. A written test that checks your ability to add, subtract, and calculate is a _____ test.

11. _____ testing is used to provide a safer work environment for employees.

How to Take Preemployment Tests

Activity E

Name _____

Chapter 17

Date _____ Period _____

Working in a small group, develop a checklist for preparing to take preemployment tests. Include the steps and tips an individual can use to prepare for success in taking preemployment tests. Use the information in the text as well as information from Internet searches, library resources, and your own experiences. Use the space below for your checklist.   (Sample responses are shown.)

1. Try to find out in advance what kind of tests you must take.

2. Practice for skill tests.

3. Get plenty of rest the night before.

4. Bring an extra pencil for written tests.

5. Arrive at the test site early.

6. Select a seat where you can see and hear the examiner well.

7. Ask questions about instructions that you do not understand.

8. Do not linger too long over one question.

9. Answer the easiest questions first.

10. Have confidence in your abilities.

Interviewing for Jobs

Learning About an Employer

Activity A

Chapter 18

Name_____

Date_____**Period**_____

Before you go on an interview, you should learn about a prospective employer. List a company for which you would like to work. Then research the company by consulting the Internet, library resources, annual reports, and other sources to find the following information.   (Answers are student response.)

1. Company name: _____

2. Describe the company's products or services. _____

   _____

   _____

   _____

   _____

   _____

   _____

   _____

   _____

   _____

   _____

   _____

   _____

3. How many people are employed by this company?_____

4. What are the possibilities for the growth and expansion of this company?_____

   _____

   _____

   _____

5. How can knowing this information help you on a job interview?_____

   _____

   _____

   _____

   _____

Interview Preparation

Activity B

Chapter 18

Name_____

Date_____**Period**_____

Make a good impression during a job interview by preparing yourself for it. Complete the following exercise on preparing for an interview.

1. List at least four questions you would like to ask the interviewer about the job and company.

   Job: _(Student response.)_____

   Company: _(Student response.)_____

   Questions:

   A. (Sample response.) Would I receive training for the job?_____

   _____

   B. (Sample response.) What hours would I work?_____

   _____

   C. (Sample response.) Are there opportunities for advancement?_____

   _____

   D. (Sample response.) May I see the work site?_____

   _____

2. List items you would take with you on this interview. _(Sample response.) résumé, portfolio, personal_

   fact sheet, list of references, black pen, two pencils, directions to the company_____

   _____

   _____

   _____

   _____

3. Imagine you have been offered the job. List at least four questions you would ask the interviewer before accepting or rejecting the job offer.

   A. (Sample response.) What is the salary?_____

   _____

   B. (Sample response.) Do you provide insurance?_____

   _____

   C. (Sample response.) Do I receive paid vacation time?_____

   _____

   D. (Sample response.) Does the company have a profit-sharing plan?_____

   _____

Deciding What to Wear

Activity C

Chapter 18

Name_____

Date_____Period_____

Suppose you are going on interviews for the jobs listed below. Describe what you would wear for each interview. (Sample responses are shown.)

1. Word processor: casual business dress—a nice shirt, pants, and tie; conservative skirt and blouse

2. Bank teller: a suit

3. Sales associate: a suit

4. Auto technician: casual business dress—a nice shirt and pants; conservative skirt and blouse

5. Receptionist: casual business dress—a nice shirt, pants, and tie; conservative skirt and blouse

6. Stock clerk: casual business dress—a nice shirt and pants; conservative skirt and blouse

7. Landscaper: a suit

8. Restaurant server: casual business dress—a nice shirt, pants, and tie; conservative skirt and blouse

9. Construction worker: casual business dress—a nice shirt and pants; conservative skirt and blouse

10. Data entry clerk: casual business dress—a nice shirt, pants, and tie; conservative skirt and blouse

11. Cashier: casual business dress—a nice shirt, pants, and tie; conservative skirt and blouse

12. Customer service representative: a suit

13. Your career goal: (Student response.)

Interview Questions

Activity D

Chapter 18

Name_____

Date_____Period_____

Before you go on an interview, it is a good idea to be prepared for the type of questions you may be asked. Questions often asked in an interview are listed below. Review each question, then answer it as you would during an interview.   (Answers are student response.)

1. Please tell me about yourself. _____
   _____
   _____

2. Why do you want to work for this company? _____
   _____

3. What were your best subjects in school? _____
   _____

4. What were your toughest subjects in school? What did you do to make good grades? _____
   _____
   _____

5. Give me an example of a complex project for which you were totally responsible. Explain what you did.
   _____
   _____

6. What do you see yourself doing in five years? _____
   _____
   _____

7. What types of jobs are you trying to avoid? _____
   _____

8. What was the toughest decision you've ever made? Explain why._____
   _____
   _____

9. What do you do when you have trouble solving a problem? _____
   _____

10. When do you like working with people and when do you prefer working alone? _____
    _____
    _____

11. What level of pay do you expect? _____
    _____

Interviewing for a Job

Activity E

Chapter 18

Name_____

Date_____Period_____

Complete the following statements about interviewing for a job by selecting the best answer. Then explain why you have chosen that answer.   (Answers for reasons will vary.)

___A___ 1. It is best to arrive for an interview _____.
   A. five to 10 minutes early
   B. exactly on time
   C. just a little late

Reason: to allow yourself a few minutes to compose yourself; to make sure you are ready when the interviewer

is ready; to demonstrate that you can be prompt

___C___ 2. Go to an interview _____.
   A. with a friend
   B. with a parent
   C. by yourself

Reason: to avoid giving the impression that you will not be comfortable working alone

___A___ 3. To hide nervousness, _____.
   A. do your best to be relaxed
   B. smoke
   C. chew gum

Reason: your body language will communicate your personality to the interviewer; chewing gum or smoking is

distracting and impolite

___C___ 4. When talking to the interviewer, _____.
   A. avoid eye contact
   B. look out the window
   C. maintain eye contact

Reason: shows you are enthusiastic about the job and interested in what the employer is saying

___B___ 5. If the interviewer asks you about your qualifications, _____.
   A. brag
   B. briefly describe your accomplishments
   C. be bashful and do not respond

Reason: brief, confident answers will communicate that you are truthful and well-prepared; being bashful may

imply that you are not confident; bragging can be offensive to the employer

___A___ 6. If you do not know the answer to a question, _____.
   A. admit it
   B. fake it
   C. try to change the subject

Reason: admitting you do not know the answer shows the interviewer that you are honest; if you lie about your

skills, it will probably become apparent from your job performance that you were lying and you could be fired

(Continued)

Name_____

_____C_____ 7. When speaking to an interviewer, _____.
      A. mumble
      B. speak softly
      C. speak clearly

Reason: speaking clearly shows you are confident; it shows you can communicate well; you want to be sure

the interviewer receives the correct information

_____B_____ 8. If you do not have the skills for a certain job, _____.
      A. fake it
      B. admit it
      C. try to change the subject

Reason: admitting you do not know the answer shows the interviewer that you are honest; if you lie about your

skills, it will probably become apparent from your job performance that you were lying and you could be fired

_____C_____ 9. If you were fired from another job, and the interviewer asks why, _____.
      A. lie about it
      B. try to change the subject
      C. admit the fact

Reason: you can try to turn it into a positive by sharing what you learned from the experience; you can demon-

strate that you take responsibility for your mistake and don't blame others

_____B_____ 10. The purpose of a job interview is to _____.
      A. brag about yourself
      B. convince the employer that you are the right person for the job
      C. beg for a job

Reason: bragging or begging may only prove that you do *not* have the right qualifications for the job

_____A_____ 11. Before accepting a job offer, you should consider _____.
      A. pay and fringe benefits
      B. how good you look in the uniform
      C. how long the interview was

Reason: pay and fringe benefits are some of the most important factors about choosing a job

_____A_____ 12. If you decide to reject a job offer, you should _____.
      A. explain why you are not accepting the offer
      B. ignore the job offer
      C. wait two weeks to inform the interviewer of your decision

Reason: the interviewer will appreciate a direct, honest answer; rejecting a job immediately allows the employer

more time to plan for interviewing other candidates

Interview Practice

Activity F

Chapter 18

Name_____

Date_____Period_____

In class, practice interviewing for a job. Have another class member role-play an employer who is interviewing you for a job. The interviewer may ask questions from Activity D or other questions appropriate for an interview. Prepare yourself as you would for an actual job interview. After completing the interview, have the interviewer evaluate you by using the following checklist. Then evaluate yourself.
(Answers are student response.)

Job for which you are interviewing: _____

Appearance	Yes	No
1. Clothing clean and well pressed	_____	_____
2. Clothing conservative in style	_____	_____
3. Body clean and odor-free	_____	_____
4. Hair trimmed, clean, and combed	_____	_____
5. Makeup, jewelry, and accessories used sparingly	_____	_____

Behavior and Poise

	Yes	No
6. Reported to interview area five minutes before scheduled interview	_____	_____
7. Greeted interviewer with a smile	_____	_____
8. Introduced self	_____	_____
9. Shook interviewer's hand	_____	_____
10. Sat only when asked to do so	_____	_____
11. Kept eye contact with interviewer	_____	_____
12. Listened carefully to what interviewer said	_____	_____
13. Considered questions carefully before answering	_____	_____
14. Spoke well of previous employers and associates	_____	_____
15. Showed desire to work	_____	_____
16. Asked questions during interview	_____	_____
17. Used proper communication skills	_____	_____

Interviewer's evaluation:_____

Your self-evaluation:

A. What were your strong points? _____

_____

B. What were your weak points? _____

_____

C. How could you improve your interviewing technique? _____

_____

Informational Interview Practice

Activity G   Name _____

Chapter 18   Date _____ Period _____

In class, select someone who is employed in a job area that interests you and conduct an informational interview. Ask the questions below during the interview to learn more about your classmate's job and employer. (Answers are student response.)

1. Where do you work? What is your job? _____

    _____

2. What qualifications are needed for this job? _____

    _____

    _____

    _____

3. Explain the career opportunities available in this job and with this employer. _____

    _____

    _____

4. Describe your typical workweek. _____

    _____

    _____

    _____

    _____

5. According to your employer, what are your most important job responsibilities? _____

    _____

    _____

    _____

    _____

6. How many employees are in your department? _____ The company? _____

7. Describe the effectiveness of your supervisor. _____

    _____

    _____

8. Describe the traits of an ideal employee. _____

    _____

    _____

    _____

    _____

The Follow-Up Letter

Activity H

Chapter 18

Name _____

Date _____ Period _____

Assume you interviewed with the company you researched in Activity A. In the space below, write a follow-up letter. Then enter the letter in a word processing document and print on 8½ × 11-inch white bond paper. (Follow-up letter is student response. Students should follow the format shown on page 376 of the text.)

_____

_____

_____

_____

_____

_____

_____

_____

_____

_____

_____

_____

_____

_____

_____

_____

_____

_____

_____

Checklist

The letter contains

_____ 1. the return address and date

_____ 2. a complete inside address

_____ 3. proper salutation

_____ 4. a brief message thanking the interviewer for his or her time

_____ 5. statement about my continued interest in the job

_____ 6. a correct closing with my signature

_____ 7. (if mailed) a postmark within two days of the interview

Fringe Benefits

Activity I   Name_____

Chapter 18   Date_____Period_____

Contact an employer in your community and ask about the fringe benefits offered to employees of the company. Answer the questions below. (Answers are student response.)

Company Name_____

1. Does the company provide employees with the types of insurance listed below? If so, how much coverage do the policies provide? What is the cost of the insurance to the employee?

Insurance	**Coverage**	**Cost**
Health	_____	_____
Dental	_____	_____
Life	_____	_____
Other	_____	_____

2. Does the employee receive paid vacation time? If yes, how many days per year are allowed? How long must the worker be an employee before being eligible to receive them?_____

_____

3. Does the company pay for days when an employee is sick and unable to work? If yes, how many days per year are allowed? How long must the worker be an employee before being eligible to receive them?

_____

4. Does the company provide a retirement plan? If yes, describe the plan. _____

_____

_____

5. Does the company have a profit sharing plan? If yes, describe the plan. _____

_____

6. Does the company give bonuses? If yes, when? _____

   How much?_____

7. Does the company have an education reimbursement program? If yes, describe the program._____

_____

_____

8. What other benefits does the company offer? _____

_____

9. Estimate the dollar value per year of all the benefits offered by this company._____

10. Do you think this company offers a good fringe benefit package? Explain. _____

_____

_____

 **Succeeding on the Job**

Terms for Success

Name_____

Date_____Period_____

Complete the following statements by filling in the blanks.

orientation   1. A new employee learns about the company's history, policies, rules, and safety procedures by attending a(n) _____.

incentive   2. A pay raise or partial payment of tuition are forms of an _____ that may be given to employees to encourage them to pursue further training.

conviction   3. Workers with a strong belief show _____.

Stress   4. _____ is a feeling of pressure, strain, or tension that results from change.

probation   5. During a(n) _____ period, a supervisor helps train a new worker and evaluates the worker's job skills, work habits, and ability to get along with coworkers.

performance   6. Job success depends a great deal on how your supervisor rates your _____ on the job.

fire   7. If an employee does not perform job responsibilities as requested, the employer may _____ the employee.

absenteeism   8. Not showing up for work on a regular basis, which is a common reason employers give for firing employees, is called _____.

promotion   9. A job _____ is an advancement that employees must earn by being productive, cooperative, dependable, and responsible on the job.

union   10. A(n) _____ is a group of workers who have formed together to voice their opinions to their employer or the employer's representatives (management).

union shop   11. In workplaces with _____ _____ agreements, all workers must join the union as a condition of employment.

open shop   12. In workplaces with _____ _____ agreements, workers are free to join or not join the union.

Collective bargaining   13. _____ _____ is the process that labor and management use to discuss what they expect from each other in the workplace.

labor contract   14. A(n) _____ _____ is an agreement that spells out the conditions for wages, benefits, job security, work hours, working conditions, and grievance procedures.

Starting a New Job

Activity B

Chapter 19

Name_____

Date_____Period_____

Answer the following questions about the first day on your job. (Answers are student response.)

1. Describe your first day on a new job. In your description, tell how you prepared for that day.

   _____

   _____

   _____

   _____

   _____

2. How did you learn about the company's policies and rules on your first day? _____

   _____

   _____

3. Who was responsible for your training? _____

   _____

4. What did you do to get along with your supervisor and coworkers? _____

   _____

   _____

5. According to company policy, how long is the probation period? _____

6. Imagine you are talking to a friend who is starting a new job. What advice would you give him or her about succeeding on the first day?_____

   _____

   _____

   _____

   _____

   _____

   _____

   _____

   _____

   _____

   _____

Workplace Conduct and Job Success

Activity C

Chapter 19

Name _____

Date _____ Period _____

Read the following statements about workers' conduct. If the statement is an example of good conduct, write *good* in the blank. If the statement is an example of bad conduct, write *bad* in the blank.

good	1. They communicate well.
bad	2. They think only of themselves.
bad	3. They don't smile often.
good	4. They accept responsibility for their actions.
bad	5. They blame others for their mistakes.
good	6. They respect others' opinions.
good	7. They don't criticize others.
bad	8. They often complain.
good	9. They get along with other people.
good	10. They praise the company and their supervisor.
good	11. They enjoy working with their coworkers.
good	12. They are usually cheerful.
bad	13. They have negative comments most of the time.
good	14. They are willing to try new tasks.
good	15. They believe in their ability to succeed.
bad	16. They are grouchy and irritable.
good	17. They are cooperative team members.

Think of a situation in which a coworker showed poor conduct. Describe the situation. Then explain how this person's conduct could affect his or her job success. (Sample response.) Annalise has an entry-level office position and finds her job boring. She wants to be promoted to a more exciting, higher-level position. She often puts off doing her work, even though others are waiting on her assignments to complete their own. She also whines to her superiors about doing boring assignments.

Explain how a change of attitude can help a person show improved conduct. (Sample response.) Annalise should complete her assignments cheerfully, promptly, and to the best of her ability. She will be proving to her superiors that she is capable of handling more advanced assignments.

Handling Job Stress

Activity D

Chapter 19

Name _____

Date _____ Period _____

Answer the following questions about handling job stress. (Answers are student response.)

1. What are three situations at work or school that you consider stressful?

   A. _____

   B. _____

   C. _____

2. What is your physical and emotional reaction to each situation?

   Physical reaction   Emotional reaction

   A. _____   _____

   B. _____   _____

   C. _____   _____

3. What are the possible causes of stress in each situation?

   A. _____

   _____

   B. _____

   _____

   C. _____

   _____

4. How did you handle each stressful situation?

   A. _____

   _____

   B. _____

   _____

   C. _____

   _____

5. What are four other ways to handle job stress effectively?

   A. _____

   B. _____

   C. _____

   D. _____

Job Satisfaction

Activity E

Chapter 19

Name_____

Date_____ Period_____

Indicate whether you agree or disagree with each statement in the chart and provide an explanation. Then complete the sentence below. (Chart answers are student response.)

Statement	Agree or Disagree	Reasons
1. I seem to be making progress in my job.		
2. I get personal satisfaction from my job.		
3. I feel I am paid adequately for the work I do.		
4. My work is challenging.		
5. There are opportunities for advancement in this job.		
6. This job offers me security.		
7. I perform a variety of work activities.		
8. This job gives me a feeling of accomplishment.		
9. This job allows me to make good use of my skills.		
10. This job allows me to make good use of my education and training.		
11. I am willing to accept responsibility.		
12. I am in the best job for me.		

To me, job satisfaction means _(Student response.)_____

_____

_____

_____

How Am I Doing?

Activity F

Chapter 19

Name _____

Date _____ Period _____

Review each question in the chart and rate your own job performance. Be honest and fair with yourself as you analyze the good and bad aspects of your work performance. Then write what you can do to change or improve. (There are no right or wrong answers.) (Chart answers are student response.)

Work Performance	Yes	Sometimes	No	Recommendations for Improvement
1. Do I get to work late?				
2. Do I have a good attendance record?				
3. Can I do my job well?				
4. Is my work high quality?				
5. Do I work well without supervision?				
6. Am I honest by not loafing or stealing company time or supplies?				
7. Am I loyal to my employer?				
8. Am I cooperative with my supervisor and my coworkers?				
9. Do I make a favorable personal impression?				
10. Do I keep myself well groomed?				
11. Do I practice safe working habits?				
12. Do I take proper care of my employer's equipment and materials?				

(Circle one.)

Overall, I rate my job performance as: Excellent   Very good   Acceptable   Fair   Poor

Changing Jobs

Activity G
Chapter 19

Name_____

Date_____Period_____

Interview someone who has changed jobs and ask that person the following questions. Then ask two questions of your own. Discuss the interview in class.   (Answers are student response.)

1. Why did you change jobs? _____

_____

_____

2. Did you take a job with a different employer? If you stayed with the same employer, was it a lateral move or promotion?_____

_____

_____

3. Do you feel you make the right decision by changing jobs? _____

_____

_____

_____

_____

_____

4. What advice would you give someone who is considering a job change? _____

_____

_____

_____

_____

_____

5. Question: _____

_____

Response:_____

_____

_____

6. Question: _____

_____

Response:_____

_____

_____

Unions

Activity H

Chapter 19

Name_____

Date_____Period_____

Interview someone who is a union member and ask that person the following questions. Then ask one question of your own. Discuss the interview in class.   (Answers are student response.)

1. Is union membership a requirement for your job? If not, why did you choose to become a union member?

_____

_____

2. Is union membership required of all employees at your job? _____

3. Of which union are you a member? _____

4. Who is your immediate union representative/leader? _____

5. How does a person become a union representative/leader?_____

_____

_____

6. How much are the union dues? _____

7. What are the benefits of union membership? _____

_____

_____

_____

8. Do you feel that the benefits of union membership are worth the cost? Explain. _____

_____

_____

_____

9. What does the union contract cover? _____

_____

_____

_____

_____

10. Question: _____

_____

Answer: _____

_____

_____

_____

Diversity and Rights in the Workplace

My Heritage

Activity A

Chapter 20

Name_____

Date_____Period_____

Interview a grandparent or another older relative. Ask the relative to recall being your age as he or she answers the following questions. Record the answers in the space provided and be prepared to discuss your interview in class. (Answers are student response.)

Name of interviewee: _____

Relationship of interviewee to me: _____

Age

Most children attended school until age _____

Children were considered grown and ready to become independent when they reached the age of _____

_____

The age at which most couples married was _____

Gender Issues

The household tasks handled by females consisted of_____

_____

_____

The household tasks handled by males consisted of _____

_____

_____

The jobs open to adult females included _____

_____

_____

The jobs open to adult males included _____

_____

_____

Only men were allowed to _____

_____

Women were expected to _____

_____

(Continued)

Name_____
(Answers are student response.)

Language

The primary language spoken at home was_____

The primary language spoken at school was_____

_____

_____

The language(s) spoken in banks, stores, and other public places was (were)_____

_____

Family, Culture, and Traditions

My birthplace is (city, state/region, and country) _____

_____

I grew up in (city, state/region, and country) _____

_____

My parents made a living by _____

_____

Besides my sisters, brothers, and parents, the family members living with us included _____

_____

The holidays and special events we always celebrated included _____

1. _____
2. _____
3. _____
4. _____
5. _____
6. _____
7. _____
8. _____

The foods always served at family gatherings included _____

_____

_____

_____

Religion

The houses of worship in my community included (List types, not specific names.)_____

_____

_____

Diversity Awareness

Activity B

Chapter 20

Name_____

Date_____Period_____

True/False: Circle *T* if the statement is true or *F* if the statement is false.

(T) F 1. Diversity involves respecting people's differences.

(T) F 2. When diversity is supported, everyone is allowed to maintain his or her individuality.

T (F) 3. Mexico is the most diverse country in the world because its population comes from every other nation.

T (F) 4. The diversity of the U.S. population is most evident in small rural towns.

(T) F 5. There is a natural tendency to seek out and stay close to people who are like yourself.

(T) F 6. Throughout history, conflicts have arisen when groups of people who are alike have tried to change those who are different.

(T) F 7. Factors that cause population differences include cultural heritage, race, gender, and religion.

(T) F 8. Cultural heritage determines what beliefs, learned behaviors, and language pass through the generations to each individual.

T (F) 9. Not all Americans are part of an ethnic group.

(T) F 10. When different cultures associate, there is the opportunity to share the best of what each has to offer.

T (F) 11. Today, assimilation is considered the best way to handle diverse populations.

(T) F 12. When employers, employees, and customers speak different languages, misunderstandings often result.

(T) F 13. Problems in the workplace may arise over off-time granted for observing the practices of one religion but not others.

T (F) 14. The number of older workers in society is quickly decreasing.

(T) F 15. Everyone is a potential candidate for some form of disability during his or her life.

T (F) 16. Companies have found that teaching employees to value workers' differences yields negative results.

T (F) 17. Employees feel more comfortable in the workplace when the emphasis is on who they are, not what they contribute.

(T) F 18. When all ideas are valued, people feel greater freedom to make suggestions and present alternative views.

(T) F 19. If sensitive issues can be raised without fear of hurting coworkers' feelings, decisions can be made faster.

(T) F 20. A diverse workforce understands a wider range of customers.

(T) F 21. Over half of all working-age women are employed outside the home.

T (F) 22. Companies can avoid conflict by having one religious display reflecting the beliefs of most people in the company.

(T) F 23. Unskilled older workers may have difficulty keeping their jobs.

(T) F 24. Disabled workers can be productive and dependable.

(T) F 25. Having a policy of accepting diversity can help a company gain public respect.

Promoting Diversity

Activity C	Name _____
Chapter 20	Date _____ Period _____

Working in small groups, accomplish the team assignment for promoting diversity described below.

> **Team assignment:** Your group is in charge of designing a program to promote diversity in the community or in one team member's workplace. Before developing a plan, check what others in similar situations are doing. You may gather this information from interviews, the Internet, and library sources. List below the top three ideas that your team considered most worthwhile and develop your program using one of them. Explain below the details of your program and how it would work.   (Answers are student response.)

What were the team's top three ideas for a diversity program? (List first the number 1 idea on which the team's program is based.)

1. _____
_____

2. _____
_____

3. _____
_____

Where would the team's diversity program be used? (Who is the target audience?) _____
_____
_____
_____

What types of printed material(s) would be used? (Describe it/them.) _____
_____
_____
_____

How would the target audience receive the program message?_____
_____
_____
_____

What signs should your team see if the plan is successful? _____
_____
_____

What might be some signs that the plan is *not* successful? _____
_____
_____

Know Your Rights

Activity D

Chapter 20

Name_____

Date_____ Period_____

Listed below are a variety of employment situations. Read each situation and answer the questions using information on workplace rights provided in the chapter. (For each, the answer to the second question is student response.)

1. Jerome was born in Uruguay to United States citizens. Jerome's family moved to Florida when he was twelve years old. After completing high school, Jerome applied for a position as welding apprentice at a local company. He was not considered for the apprentice position because of his birth location. The employer was unsure of Jerome's citizenship status.

   What federal law or guidelines cover this situation? Immigration Reform and Control Act of 1986

   What is the first thing Jerome should do? (Sample response.) Jerome should find out if his birth was registered at the U.S. embassy or consulate in Uruguay to easily prove his citizenship.

2. Amanda is an entry-level software engineer at a large company. After overhearing a conversation involving her boss, Amanda discovered that her starting salary was $2,000 less than a man who held a similar position. Both positions had the same requirements regarding skill and responsibility.

   What federal law or guidelines cover this situation? Equal Pay Act of 1963

   What is the first thing Amanda should do? (Sample response.) Amanda should confront her boss about why she would be making so much less than her coworker.

3. Tracey, who works at a busy office processing mortgage applications, is paid minimum wage. Often customers call just before closing time, which forces Tracey to work after her assigned 40 hours. Tracey has been frustrated when she receives her weekly paycheck because she is paid only for 40 hours.

   What federal law or guidelines cover this situation? Fair Labor Standards Act of 1938

   What is the first thing Tracy should do? (Sample response.) Tracey should talk to her boss about the situation, since she should be receiving overtime pay.

4. Maya wears a small dot on her forehead. The dot is a symbol worn by female members of her religion. Her employer has asked her to cover the dot when she is working at the front counter assisting customers.

   What federal law or guidelines cover this situation? Civil Rights Act of 1964

   What is the first thing Maya should do? (Sample response.) Maya should inform her employer that under the law, she is engaged in religious expression that does not cause her employer undue hardship.

(Continued)

Name_____

5. Heidi applied by phone for a position at a nearby clothing store for a part-time position during the Christmas season. The ad in the paper stated that no experience was necessary. Heidi spoke to the person responsible for hiring over the phone and felt she had an excellent chance at employment. When Heidi arrived at the store in her wheelchair to complete the application, the spokesperson said all positions were filled. The next week, Heidi saw another ad in the local newspaper for employment opportunities at that same store. She felt she might not have been hired because of her disability.

What federal law or guidelines cover this situation? _Americans with Disabilities Act of 1990_

_____

What is the first thing Heidi should do? _(Sample response.) Heidi should go to the store with the ad and_

ask to speak to the spokesperson about why she was not given a fair chance at employment. She should

point out that her disability does not prevent her from doing the job described.

6. Allie works in the service department of an automobile dealership. In the break room, posters and calendars are posted showing women in swimsuits. Allie feels uncomfortable going into the break room because of these pictures. Usually when she passes through the break room, her coworkers comment on her figure and suggest a job as a calendar swimsuit model. Allie does not want any further discussion about it.

What federal law or guidelines cover this situation? _Equal Employment Opportunity Commission_

(EEOC) guidelines

What is the first thing Allie should do? _(Sample response.) Allie should inform her employer that the_

inappropriate pictures and comments are hostile environment harassment, and she wants it stopped.

_____

7. Francesca's native language is Spanish. She was excited to find a coworker from the Caribbean at her place of employment. At breaks and lunch, Francesca and her new friend speak in Spanish to each other. Francesca's supervisor has requested Francesca to only speak English at work because other coworkers feel uncomfortable hearing a different language.

What federal law or guidelines cover this situation? _Equal Employment Opportunity Commission_

(EEOC) guidelines

What is the first thing Francesca should do? _(Sample response.) Francesca should point out to her supervisor_

that under EEOC guidelines, she is allowed to speak whatever language she wants as long as it does not interfere

with her job. The language she speaks during breaks and lunch cannot interfere with her job performance.

8. At age 55, Leona is looking for a new job. She was laid off from her job at a telephone company where she received numerous awards for outstanding work during her twenty years in the accounting department. Leona is becoming very discouraged in her job search after receiving ten rejection letters this week. She thinks that her age is the reason for a lack of job offers. She also thinks her layoff from the telephone company was due to her age.

What federal law or guidelines cover this situation? _Age Discrimination in Employment Act of 1967_

_____

What is the first thing Leona should do? _(Sample response.) Leona should file a charge with the EEOC_

against the telephone company. She can present her awards and performance reviews as documentation.

The EEOC will decide if she should pursue a case against them.

Diversity Terms

Activity E

Chapter 20

Name_____

Date_____Period_____

Complete the following word puzzle by filling in the correct terms. Then answer the question at the bottom of the page and discuss your answer in class.

1 G E N D E R
2 C R I M I N A L
3 C I V I L
4 A G E
5 D I S C R I M I N A T I O N
6 A S S I M I L A T I O N
7 R A C I S M
8 E T H N I C
9 S T E R E O T Y P E

1. Women face sex discrimination, or _____ bias, when they are restricted from training opportunities and higher-paying jobs.

2. _____ penalties, including a jail sentence or fine, may result from interfering with a person's employment rights.

3. The 1964 _____ Rights Act banned employment discrimination on the basis of race, color, religion, sex, or national origin.

4. The across-the-board firing of people over 40 to allow younger, less costly employees to fill the jobs is an example of _____ discrimination.

5. Treating people on a basis other than individual merit.

6. Blending people into society by helping, and sometimes forcing, them to become more like the majority.

7. The belief that one race is superior or inferior to all others.

8. A group of people who share common racial and/or cultural characteristics is a(n) _____ group.

9. A label given to a person based on assumptions held about all members of that person's racial or cultural group.

10. What strategies are used at your school or workplace to promote diversity?

(Student response.) _____

_____

_____

_____

_____

_____

Harassment Points

Activity F

Chapter 20

Name_____

Date_____Period_____

Fill in the chart below using the information about sexual harassment in your text.
(Sample responses are shown.)

5 things I know about harassment:	**4** things that discourage harassment:	**3** actions to take when harassment happens:
1. includes unwelcome and unwanted advances	1. Familiarize yourself with your right to a workplace free of illegal behavior.	1. Tell the aggressor to stop.
2. can be verbal or physical	2. Know your company's policy and reporting procedure.	2. Keep detailed records.
3. victim and aggressor can be either sex	3. Be businesslike at all times.	3. Report the offense.
4. primarily an issue of power	4. Clearly let the aggressor know that you want the offensive conduct to stop.	
5. types include quid pro quo and hostile environment		

Succeeding in Our Economic System

Another Economic System

Activity A	**Name**_____
Chapter 21	**Date**_____ **Period**_____

Interview someone who has lived under an economic system that is different from the free enterprise system of the United States. (A foreign exchange student could be a good resource person.) Find out the following information. Discuss the interview in class. (Sample responses are shown.)

1. Person interviewed: _(Name)_____

2. Country:_ India _____

3. Type of economic system:_ Mixed economy (socialist and capitalist) _____

4. Describe life under the economic system of this person's country:_ India's formerly socialist economy _
   has gradually shifted to become more capitalist. Important areas, such as railways and the postal system,
   remain under government control. The majority of the people earn their income through agriculture.
   _____
   _____
   _____
   _____
   _____
   _____
   _____

5. Describe the major differences between this economic system and the free enterprise system of the
   United States:_ India is still classified as having a low-income economy. Until the early 1990s, India was _
   largely isolated from foreign trade, but imported far more than it exported. Since government control over
   trade has lessened, India has gradually become less dependent on foreign countries. In the past, most banks
   were nationalized, or under government control. Today, many banks are privately owned.
   _____
   _____
   _____
   _____
   _____
   _____
   _____

Business in a Free Enterprise System

Activity B   **Name**_____

Chapter 21   **Date**_____**Period**_____

Interview a business owner to find answers to the following questions. Discuss your findings in class.
(Interview answers are student response.)

1. Name of business: _____

2. Is this business a proprietorship, partnership, or corporation? _____

3. How long has the business existed? _____

4. What does this business produce or what service does it provide?_____
   _____
   _____

5. How does supply and demand affect this business? _____
   _____
   _____
   _____
   _____

6. What competitors does this business have?_____
   _____
   _____

7. How does this business compete?_____
   _____
   _____

8. In what way is the government involved with this business (through controls, regulations, etc.)? _____
   _____
   _____

9. What is the structure of this business? Describe it. _____
   _____
   _____

10. How many employees (part-time and full-time) work here? _____
    _____

11. What outside consultants, such as accountants and attorneys, are used?_____
    _____
    _____
    _____

The Competitive Business World

Activity C

Chapter 21

Name_____

Date_____ Period_____

Competition encourages businesses to make quality goods and services available at lower prices. Working with a small group, research the price of a handheld global positioning navigation system (GPS) from four different sources. Include a local business, mail-order catalog, and Web site in your search. Then answer the questions below. Compare your findings with other teams in your class.

Features desired in GPS system: (Student response.)

Source	Price	Additional Charges	Delivery Time
1. (Student response.)			
2. (Student response.)			
3. (Student response.)			
4. (Student response.)			

Where is the best place to purchase the GPS? (Student response.)

Why? (Student response.)

What factors affect the costs of the GPS? (Answers will vary.) supply and demand, advancement of technology, different features

How do supply and demand affect the cost of the GPS? (Sample response.) When most people have a GPS, the demand and the cost will go down. When newer GPS systems with better technology are released, the demand and the cost will be high.

In the next five years, from which source do you think most people will purchase a GPS system? Explain. (Sample response.) In the next five years, GPS may become a standard feature on vehicles, so most may be purchased from car dealerships.

Free Enterprise System

Activity D

Chapter 21

Name_____

Date_____ Period_____

Match each definition below with the correct term from the word bank.

Word Bank

capital	free market	productive
competition	government	profit
corporation	monopoly	proprietorship
demand	needs	supply

_____profit_____ 1. The desire for _____ motivates businesses to produce the goods and services consumers want.

_____monopoly_____ 2. A _____ is a single company that controls the entire supply of a product or service.

_____Capital_____ 3. _____, labor, land, and equipment are productive resources used to produce and provide goods and services.

_____Competition_____ 4. _____ encourages businesses to produce quality goods and services at low prices.

_____supply_____ 5. The amount of products and services available for sale is called the _____.

_____needs_____ 6. The basics a person must have to live are called _____.

_____demand_____ 7. The total amount of products and services consumers want to buy is called _____.

_____free market_____ 8. In a _____, people have the right to decide how and where to earn, spend, save, and invest their money.

_____government_____ 9. Some _____ involvement is required to keep our economic system free and fair.

_____Productive_____ 10. _____ resources are all resources used to produce goods and services.

_____proprietorship_____ 11. A business that has only one owner is a _____.

_____corporation_____ 12. A _____ is a business owned by many people that have purchased stock in the company.

Forms of Business Ownership

Activity E

Chapter 21

Name_____

Date_____Period_____

In the following statements, match the form of business ownership with the appropriate description. Then fill the chart below with examples from your community. Name two businesses for each form of ownership listed. Be prepared to explain your decisions to the class.

____C____ 1. Steven is a stockholder in an international oil company.

____B____ 2. When Mary Elman died, the business she and Veronica Glass owned jointly was dissolved.

____A____ 3. Lee Clausen operates a fast-food business specializing in submarine sandwiches. Lee receives all the profits that are made.

____A____ 4. Randy Grier's interest in baseball player cards evolved into a small business out of his home.

____B____ 5. Although she does not work with her friend, Barbara invested money in her friend's beauty salon.

____C____ 6. Dave's company plans to expand the business and produce more goods by selling stocks to investors.

____A____ 7. Al's interest and experience in woodworking and art led him to start his own retail framing business.

____B____ 8. Marta and her brother plan to operate their father's dry cleaning business after his retirement.

A. sole proprietorship
B. partnership
C. corporation

Businesses in the Community	
Type of Ownership	**Name**
Proprietorship	1. (Student response.)
	2. (Student response.)
Partnership	1. (Student response.)
	2. (Student response.)
Corporation	1. (Student response.)
	2. (Student response.)

Business Structures

Activity F

Chapter 21

Name_____

Date_____ Period_____

Prepare an organization chart showing the management structure that exists where you work (or at your school). Begin with the top managerial position and show the organizational levels down through lower-level employees. Explain the structure in class.   (Organization chart is student response. Students should follow the format provided on page 437 of the text.)

Employer's name: _____

Type of management structure:_____

(Diagram of business structure:)

Entrepreneurship: A Business of Your Own

Importance of Small Business

Name_____

Date_____Period_____

Read the following statements about small businesses. If the statement is true, circle *T*. If it is false, circle *F* and rewrite the statement on the line below to make it true.

(T) F 1. Businesses owned by entrepreneurs help keep the economy strong by creating jobs.

_____

_____

T (F) 2. Small businesses compete only against small corporations.

(Small businesses compete against corporations of all sizes.)_____

_____

(T) F 3. The overall standard of living increases when more people work.

_____

_____

T (F) 4. Small businesses employ a third of all U.S. workers not employed by government.

(Small businesses employ the majority of U.S. workers not employed by government.)_____

_____

(T) F 5. Some small businesses provide specialized products that large corporations do not.

_____

_____

T (F) 6. The economy of the United States does *not* rely on small business owners.

(Small business owners help keep the economy strong by creating jobs.)_____

_____

T (F) 7. Small businesses account for few of the innovative products and services.

(Small businesses account for the majority of innovative products and services.)_____

_____

(T) F 8. Small businesses help keep prices in line.

_____

_____

Exploring Entrepreneurship

Name_____

Date_____Period_____

Interview an entrepreneur in your community. Find out the answers to the questions below. Write two additional questions of your own. Discuss the interview in class. (Interview answers are student response.)

Name of entrepreneur: _____

Name of business: _____

1. What product or service do you sell? Explain why you decided to work in this type of business. _____
   _____
   _____

2. How long have you been in business? _____

3. How did you start the business? _____
   _____
   _____

4. What personal skill or knowledge is most needed to start this type of business?_____
   _____

5. What form of business ownership do you have now? _____

6. Why did you choose to locate your business in its present location? _____
   _____
   _____

7. How many hours do you work weekly?_____

8. What do you see as the greatest advantage of having your own business? _____
   _____

9. What do you dislike most about being your own boss? _____
   _____

10. Question: _____
    Response:_____
    _____
    _____

11. Question: _____
    Response:_____
    _____
    _____

Qualities for Success

Activity C

Chapter 22

Name _____

Date _____ Period _____

Do you have what it takes to succeed as an entrepreneur? Listed below are some of the qualities successful entrepreneurs possess. Place a check mark next to the qualities you believe you possess. Then answer the questions that follow. (Answers are student response.)

Qualities I Possess:

_____

_____

_____

_____

_____

_____

Motivating Goals

- to pursue a dream
- to make noteworthy achievements
- to be profitable
- to have total control
- to use all skills and talents
- to surpass the efforts of peers

Personality

_____

_____

_____

_____

_____

_____

- self-starter
- self-assured
- outgoing
- efficient
- risk-taker
- optimistic

Aptitudes/Abilities

_____

_____

_____

_____

_____

_____

- sets goals and makes plans
- innovative
- organized
- solves problems well
- people-oriented
- understands basic financial matters

1. What do you feel are the most important qualities for an entrepreneur to have? _____

_____

_____

_____

_____

(Continued)

Name_____
(Answers are student response.)

2. Would you like to be an entrepreneur? Explain._____
   _____
   _____
   _____
   _____

3. Who are entrepreneurs in your community? List their names and describe their businesses._____
   _____
   _____
   _____
   _____
   _____
   _____
   _____
   _____
   _____
   _____
   _____
   _____

4. Considering your interests, abilities, and work experiences, what type of business might you like to run?
   _____
   _____
   _____
   _____
   _____
   _____

5. How would you evaluate your likelihood of becoming an entrepreneur? Place a check next to the one statement that best describes your evaluation.

   _____ I definitely want to have my own business in the future.

   _____ I am very interested in starting a business, but I need more experience first.

   _____ I am not interested in starting my own business, but I could change my mind.

   _____ I want to work for an established employer.

Planning a Business

Activity D

Chapter 22

Name _____

Date _____ Period _____

Suppose you want to become an entrepreneur. To help you start planning this business, complete the following information. Then report your business plan to the class. (Answers are student response.)

1. Describe the business you would start. _____

   _____

   _____

   _____

   _____

2. Identify the product or service your business would offer. _____

   _____

   _____

   _____

   _____

3. List your skills and experience that relate to the business. _____

   _____

   _____

   _____

4. Indicate the potential success for the business. (Consider potential customers, the competition, and your sales ability.) _____

   _____

   _____

   _____

5. Indicate a location for the business. _____

   _____

6. What factors would you consider in establishing a price for your product or service? _____

   _____

   _____

   _____

7. What form of business structure would you choose? Why? _____

   _____

   _____

   _____

(Continued)

Name _____
(Answers are student response.)

8. Identify any zoning laws that would regulate your business operation. _____

_____

_____

_____

_____

9. Identify governmental licenses or permits needed. _____

_____

_____

10. Explain how you would obtain financing to get a business started. _____

_____

_____

11. Indicate the capital expenses needed to start the business. (Consider equipment and supplies you will need.)

_____

_____

_____

_____

_____

12. What type of record-keeping system would you use? Why? _____

_____

_____

13. What professional assistance would you seek to help start and operate the business? _____

_____

_____

_____

14. What weaknesses in your plan could cause the business to fail?_____

_____

_____

_____

15. What strengths in your plan could make the business a success? _____

_____

_____

_____

_____

(Continued)

Name_____

(Business plan is student response. Students may refer to
www.sba.gov/smallbusinessplanner/plan/writeabusinessplan/index.html.)

16. Using your responses from questions 2 through 11, develop a start-up business plan.

My Business Plan

_____

_____

_____

_____

_____

_____

_____

_____

_____

_____

_____

_____

_____

_____

_____

_____

_____

_____

_____

_____

_____

_____

_____

_____

_____

_____

_____

_____

_____

_____

Entrepreneurship Terms

Activity E

Chapter 22

Name_____

Date_____Period_____

Complete each sentence by using a term from the word bank.

Word Bank

assets	fixed	innovative	overhead
break-even point	flexible	liabilities	profit ratio
capital	franchise	loan	receipts
commission	fraud	location	zoning laws

_____receipts_____ 1. Your _____ include all the money you receive from your customers for cash and credit sales.

_____Capital_____ 2. _____ expenses are one-time costs needed to get the business started.

_____assets_____ 3. Items that a business owns are called _____.

_____innovative_____ 4. The ability to come up with new ideas is being _____.

_____location_____ 5. The _____ of a business could determine the success of the business.

_____Zoning laws_____ 6. _____ _____ regulate what types of business activities can be performed in certain areas.

_____loan_____ 7. When planning a business, you would need to contact a financial institution to arrange for a(n) _____.

_____franchise_____ 8. A(n) _____ is the right to market another company's product or service.

_____commission_____ 9. A(n) _____ is a percentage of sales paid to a salesperson.

_____fixed_____ 10. Examples of _____ expenses would be monthly rent payments and garbage pickup.

_____fraud_____ 11. People who rush into businesses are prime victims of franchise and business _____.

_____overhead_____ 12. Rent, utilities, office supplies, postage, and advertising are all examples of _____ expenses.

_____Flexible_____ 13. _____ expenses are those that vary from month to month.

_____break-even point_____ 14. The _____-_____ _____ is when the income of a business equals expenses.

_____liabilities_____ 15. Any debts that you owe are called _____.

_____profit ratio_____ 16. Your _____ _____ is the percentage of your receipts that are profit.

Understanding Income and Taxes

Forms of Income

Name_____

Date_____Period_____

Read the statements below and write the missing terms in the crossword puzzle.

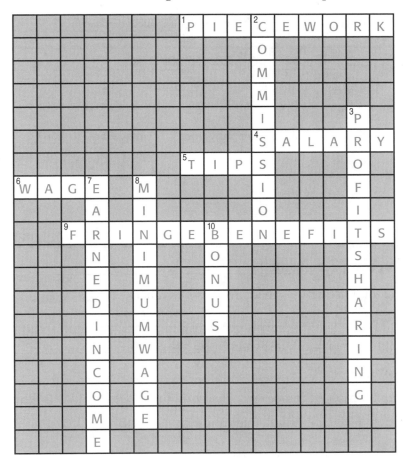

Across

1. A fixed amount of money for each piece of work done.
4. A set amount of money paid for a certain period of time.
5. Small amounts of money given by customers to service-related workers in return for good service.
6. A set amount of pay for every hour worked.
9. Extra financial rewards, such as holidays, sick leave, and profit sharing. (two words)

Down

2. A percentage of money taken in from sales made.
3. Profits returned to employees who create greater profit for the company through their hard work. (two words)
7. Money you receive for doing a job. (two words)
8. The lowest amount of money an employer is allowed by law to pay per hour. (two words)
10. An extra payment in addition to a worker's regular pay.

Understanding Your Paycheck

Activity B   Name _____

Chapter 23   Date _____ Period _____

Stephen works full-time during the summer at a local fast-food restaurant. He just received his first pay-check. Use the paycheck stub below to answer the following questions about his paycheck.

1. Identify the important parts of his paycheck in the space provided.

A. _gross pay_____   B. _deductions_____   C. _net pay_____

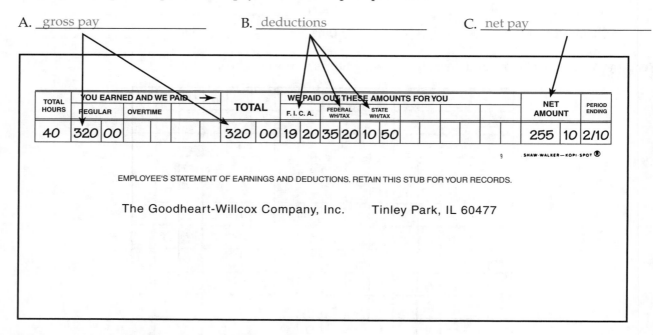

TOTAL HOURS	YOU EARNED AND WE PAID → REGULAR	OVERTIME		TOTAL	WE PAID OUT THESE AMOUNTS FOR YOU F.I.C.A.	FEDERAL WH/TAX	STATE WH/TAX				NET AMOUNT	PERIOD ENDING
40	320 00			320 00	19 20	35 20	10 50				255 10	2/10

9   SHAW·WALKER—KOPI·SPOT ®

EMPLOYEE'S STATEMENT OF EARNINGS AND DEDUCTIONS. RETAIN THIS STUB FOR YOUR RECORDS.

The Goodheart-Willcox Company, Inc.   Tinley Park, IL 60477

2. What was Stephen's gross pay? _$320.00_____

3. How much were the total deductions made from his paycheck? _$64.90_____

4. What was Stephen's net pay? _$255.10_____

5. How many hours did Stephen work last week? __40 hours_____

6. What is his hourly wage? _$8.00_____

7. When Stephen started his job, his employer asked him to fill out Form W-4. Why? _The W-4 Form tells_ _Stephen's employer how much tax to withhold from his paycheck._

8. Stephen is single and is claimed on his parents' tax return as an exemption. Can Stephen claim himself as an exemption on his Form W-4? Explain. _No, Stephen cannot claim a personal exemption for himself_ _on his Form W-4 because his parents claim him as a dependent on their tax return._

9. What social security taxes were deducted? _____$19.20_____

10. What other types of deductions could be taken out of Stephen's paycheck? _insurance premiums, union_ _dues, charitable contributions, and contributions to a retirement plan and/or savings plan_

Types of Taxes

Activity C

Chapter 23

Name_____

Date_____Period_____

Five types of taxes are listed below. Match each type of tax to its description. (The types of taxes may be used more than once. There may be more than one answer for each description.)

__A, B__ 1. A tax on a person's income.

__E__ 2. A tax placed on certain products such as gasoline or cigarettes.

__A, C, D__ 3. Examples of direct taxes.

__D__ 4. A tax on goods and services.

__A__ 5. An example of a progressive tax.

__A, B__ 6. Taxes withheld from a paycheck by an employer, as determined by the information provided on the Employee's Withholding Allowance Certificate by the employee.

__E__ 7. A tax placed on certain products or services such as telephone service or liquor.

__D__ 8. In some states, food and drugs may be exempt from this tax.

__E__ 9. This tax is an example of an indirect tax.

__D__ 10. This tax is an example of a regressive tax.

A. personal income tax
B. social security tax
C. property tax
D. sales tax
E. excise tax

Tax Opinions

Activity D

Chapter 23

Name_____

Date_____Period_____

For each statement below, indicate whether you agree or disagree by circling one of the terms. Explain your decisions and be prepared to discuss your opinions with the class. (There are no right or wrong answers.) (Answers are student response.)

1. Income tax is the fairest tax. (Agree, Disagree) Explain. _____
   _____
   _____
   _____

2. A sales tax is not fair to some groups in a community. (Agree, Disagree) Explain. _____
   _____
   _____
   _____
   _____

3. An excise tax on gasoline is a fair tax. (Agree, Disagree) Explain._____
   _____
   _____
   _____
   _____

4. Everyone should pay the same taxes regardless of their income level. (Agree, Disagree) Explain. _____
   _____
   _____
   _____
   _____

5. The government makes good use of our tax dollars. (Agree, Disagree) Explain. _____
   _____
   _____
   _____
   _____

6. Paying taxes is necessary so the government can operate smoothly. (Agree, Disagree) Explain. _____
   _____
   _____
   _____

Preparing Tax Returns

Activity E

Chapter 23

Name _____

Date _____ Period _____

Answer the following questions.

1. Joel works at his uncle's sporting goods store, volunteering a few hours a week to help keep financial records straight. Is he required to file a federal income tax return? Explain. _No. Joel volunteers his time_ _and is not a wage earner._

2. Too much tax was withheld from Cheryl's paychecks during the year. What will happen when she files her federal income tax return? _Cheryl will get a refund._

3. Not enough tax was withheld from Larry's paycheck during the year. What will happen when Larry files his federal income tax return? _Larry will be required to pay additional money to the federal_ _government._

4. Which of the following must you list as income on your tax return? Check the correct answer(s). _____

   __✓__ wages   __✓__ tips   __✓__ salaries   __✓__ bonuses

5. Lisa is preparing her federal income tax return. What is a legal way she can avoid paying some or all of her taxes? _by claiming legitimate deductions, adjustments, and credits_

6. Roy failed to declare all his income and falsified his deductions, adjustments, and credits on his income tax return. What has Roy committed? _tax evasion, which is a criminal offense_

7. Steve wants to get extra copies of federal income tax return forms. Where can he obtain them? _from_ _post offices, most banks and libraries, and the Internal Revenue Service_

8. What financial records might Marsha need in order to file an accurate federal income tax return? _____
   records of income including wages, tips, and taxable benefits; records of interest earned and dividends
   received; canceled checks for expenses entered on tax returns as deductions; records of interest paid on a
   home mortgage; past tax returns

Government Insurance Programs

Activity F

Chapter 23

Name_____

Date_____ Period_____

Complete the following statements by filling in the blanks.

Social Security _____ 1. The federal government's program for providing income when a family's earnings are reduced or stopped because of retirement, disability, or death is called _____ _____.

basic _____ 2. The purpose of social security is to provide a(n) _____ level of income that people can build on with savings, pensions, investments, or other insurance.

credits _____ 3. You must have earned a certain number of social security _____ before you can receive social security benefits.

62 _____ 4. Workers may retire as early as age _____, but they will receive lower retirement benefits.

67 _____ 5. Workers born after 1959 become eligible for full retirement benefits at age _____.

disability _____ 6. A worker who becomes severely disabled before age 65 can receive _____ checks.

survivors' _____ 7. If a worker dies, _____ benefits can be paid to certain members of the worker's family.

apply _____ 8. When a person becomes eligible for social security benefits, he or she must _____ for them at the nearest social security office.

percentage _____ 9. The social security tax is figured as a(n) _____ of an employee's income.

Supplemental Security Income 10. _____ _____ _____ pays benefits to individuals with disabilities who have few possessions or little money.

Medicare _____ 11. The _____ program was created to provide older citizens and people with disabilities with affordable health insurance.

Medicaid _____ 12. The _____ program was created to provide health care services to low-income people who are unable to pay for them.

workers' compensation _____ 13. The _____ _____ program was created to provide payments to workers if they are injured on the job.

rehabilitation _____ 14. Under workers' compensation, _____ programs provide funding for retraining workers who must give up their jobs because of injury.

Unemployment insurance 15. _____ _____ provides benefits to workers who have lost their jobs through no fault of their own.

Managing Spending

Managing Your Money

Name_____

Date_____ Period_____

Complete the following open-ended statements about budgeting your money and being an informed consumer. (Answers are student response.)

1. Now that I'm earning an income, I plan to_____

_____

_____

2. In the future, I want to be able to buy _____

_____

_____

3. To make the most of the dollars I earn, I _____

_____

_____

4. Of the many possible forms of payment (cash, checks, credit cards, etc.), I tend to use _____

_____

5. If I see something I want to buy but do not have enough cash, I would probably_____

_____

6. When I buy a product or service that does not live up to the claims advertised, I _____

_____

7. To me, a budget is_____

_____

8. The definition of a smart shopper is _____

_____

_____

9. The shopping advice I carefully listen to is _____

_____

10. An example of the type of shopping advice I ignore is _____

_____

Fixed and Flexible Expenses

Activity B

Chapter 24

Name_____

Date_____Period_____

Complete the following exercise about fixed and flexible expenses.

1. Define *fixed expenses*. _Fixed expenses are the expenses that must be paid regularly. They are payments_ _you have contracted._

_____

2. Define *flexible expenses*. _Flexible expenses are expenses you have for which you pay varying amounts._

_____

_____

3. The following items could appear on your budget. Indicate those items that are fixed expenses and those that are flexible expenses by placing a check in the appropriate column.

Products and Services	Fixed Expenses	Flexible Expenses
Bus fare		✓
Books		✓
Car repair		✓
Doctor bill		✓
Groceries		✓
Insurance premium	✓	
Medicine		✓
Movie		✓
Raincoat		✓
Rent	✓	
Savings		✓
Car payment	✓	
Phone bill		✓
Bowling		✓
Summer school		✓

Preparing a Budget

Activity C

Chapter 24

Name_____

Date_____Period_____

Prepare a monthly budget for yourself. Then evaluate the budget. You may use the form below or prepare your own on a separate sheet of paper.   (Answers are student response.)

Monthly Budget		
Goals	Approximate Cost	Date to achieve goal
Short-range _____	$_____	_____
_____	_____	_____
Long-range _____	_____	_____
_____	_____	_____

Income		**Fixed Expenses**	
		Description	Amount
Salary	$_____	_____	$_____
Interest on savings	_____	_____	_____
Interest on investments	_____	_____	_____
Part-time work	_____		_____
Other	_____	**Flexible Expenses**	
	_____	_____	_____
	_____	_____	_____
	_____	_____	_____
	_____	_____	_____
Total Income:	$_____	**Total Expenses:**	$_____

1. Do you have enough income to cover your expenses?_____
2. Is the budget flexible enough to handle unexpected expenses?_____
3. Is your money doing what you want it to do?_____
4. Is your budget helping you reach important goals on schedule?_____
5. If you answered *no* to any of the questions above, what changes should you make in your budget? ____

_____
_____
_____

Advertising

Activity D

Chapter 24

Name _____

Date _____ Period _____

Use the Internet, newspapers, and magazines to find advertisements for the products and services listed below. For each advertisement, place a check in the appropriate column to indicate the promotional method used. Then answer the questions that follow.   (Checkmarks are student response.)

	Special Sales	Promotions	Buying Incentives
Food			
Clothing			
Furniture			
Photo printing			
Automobile			
Hair or nail care			
Phone service			
Electronic equipment			

1. What is the purpose of advertising?

   to sell goods and services _____

   _____

2. Do any of your advertisements appear misleading? If so, explain how. (Student response.) _____

   _____

   _____

   _____

   _____

3. Did any of the ads try to persuade you to buy products or services you do not need, do not want, or cannot afford? If so, which? (Student response.) _____

   _____

   _____

4. How can consumers use ads to make wise buying decisions? Consumers learn more about the goods

   and services available to them. They can compare products and prices. _____

   _____

   _____

   _____

Where to Shop?

Activity E

Chapter 24

Name_____

Date_____Period_____

Several products are listed in the chart below. Decide where you would prefer to shop for each product. Place a check in the appropriate column to indicate your choice. Then answer the questions that follow. (Answers are student response.)

Products:	Department Store	Discount Store	Specialty Store	Factory Outlet	Catalog Mail-Order/TV	Direct Mail	Internet
Fashionable clothing							
Greeting cards							
Brand-name running shoes							
Perfume or cologne							
Microwave oven							
Prom dress or tuxedo rental							
Desk							
School supplies							

1. Choose three products from the chart above. Explain what factors affected your shopping decisions for each.

    A. _____

    _____

    _____

    B. _____

    _____

    _____

    C. _____

    _____

    _____

2. Of the many types of shopping sites available, which type do you prefer? Explain. _____

    _____

    _____

    _____

Comparison Shopping

Activity F

Chapter 24

Name_____

Date_____ Period_____

Comparison shopping helps you save money, get better quality, and find the products that best suit your needs. Select one item you would like to purchase. Comparison shop in three different stores. Complete the chart below with your shopping information. Then answer the questions that follow.
(Chart is student response.)

Item:_____

	Location 1	Location 2	Location 3
Name of store	_____	_____	_____
Location/site	_____	_____	_____
Price of item	_____	_____	_____
Key features (model number, brand, etc.)	_____	_____	_____
	_____	_____	_____
	_____	_____	_____
	_____	_____	_____
	_____	_____	_____
Quality	_____	_____	_____
Selection	_____	_____	_____
Customer services available	_____	_____	_____
Warranty	_____	_____	_____

1. Using the information from your chart, where would you purchase the item? (Student response.)

   _____

   Explain your choice. (Student response.)

   _____

   _____

   _____

   _____

2. How does comparison shopping help you avoid impulse buying? When you comparison shop, you plan your purchases in advance. Therefore, you do not make a purchase without thought.

   _____

   _____

   _____

The Right Way to Complain

Activity G

Chapter 24

Name _____

Date _____ Period _____

For each statement below, circle *T* if it is true or *F* if it is false.

(T) F   1. When a product or service is not satisfactory, you have the right to recourse.

T (F)   2. If you drop your new camera and break it, you have the right to complain.

T (F)   3. If you discover a problem with a purchase, it is best to wait several weeks before contacting the seller or manufacturer.

(T) F   4. If your problem cannot be settled by a store manager, you should write a letter to the company's consumer affairs department.

T (F)   5. A threatening letter is more likely to get results.

(T) F   6. At the close of a complaint letter, you should state what you would like done about the problem.

(T) F   7. If you fail to get satisfactory results from your complaint, you may need to contact an appropriate consumer organization or government agency for help.

T (F)   8. A consumer organization can force a business to accept the solution it recommends.

(T) F   9. The Better Business Bureau (BBB) is a nonprofit organization sponsored by private businesses.

(T) F   10. The BBB tries to settle consumer complaints against local businesses.

T (F)   11. The BBB *cannot* release information on other consumer complaints against a business.

(T) F   12. A consumer action group consists of a panel of people who try to judge your complaint fairly.

(T) F   13. Government agencies have the authority to take action against dishonest businesses.

T (F)   14. Federal agencies oversee the licensing of service facilities such as hospitals or nursing homes.

(T) F   15. The CPSC can require a product recall on products found to be dangerous.

T (F)   16. The CPSC regulates the production, packaging, and labeling of cosmetics.

T (F)   17. The FDA helps prevent unfair competition, deceptive trade practices, and false advertising.

(T) F   18. Problems with mail orders, warranties, and deceptive advertising can be referred to the FTC.

(T) F   19. Problems with phone, TV, and cable operators can be referred to the FCC.

(T) F   20. Filing a lawsuit should be the last resort for settling a complaint.

Complaint Letter

Activity H

Chapter 24

Name_____

Date_____ Period_____

Assume you are the consumer in the case described below. Using the facts given, compose a complaint letter to send to the store's general manager, Ms. Nakisha Jones. Write only the salutation and body of that letter in the box. (Sample response.)

Case Study: On June 16, 20xx, you purchased a cell phone for $199.00. When the salesperson demonstrated the phone in the store, the reception was excellent, but at home it was poor. You returned the cell phone for a refund on the following day to the store manager on duty, Mr. Sydney Washington. You explained the reason for the return, but Mr. Washington checked the phone and said it was fine. He refused to refund your money or exchange the cell phone. You are unhappy with the cell phone and your problem has not been settled.

Dear Ms. Jones:

On June 16, 20xx, I purchased a cell phone from your store for $199.00. When the salesperson demonstrated the phone in the store, the reception was fine. However, once I got the phone home, the reception was poor. I tried to return the phone for a refund on June 17, but the store manager, Mr. Sydney Washington, refused to refund my money or exchange the phone. I am very unhappy with the phone and would like a refund.

I will look forward to hearing from you. I appreciate your prompt attention to this problem.

Complaint Form

Activity I	Name _____
Chapter 24	Date _____ Period _____

When a product you have purchased is not satisfactory, you have the right to recourse. Imagine you are the consumer in the case below. Complete the following form using the information given.

Case Study: On February 10, 20xx, you purchased an MP3 player at Super Items, 111 South Adams Street, Anytown, IL 33614. It was advertised in your local newspaper on February 8. The advertised features included "easy to operate," 8GB built-in memory, battery life up to 22 hours for music playback, and "satisfaction guaranteed." You bought it for the advertised price of $199.99. Later at home, you found the navigation screen difficult to operate. That same day, you returned the MP3 player for a refund to Mr. Mike Hensley, the store manager on duty. You pointed out the problem, but Mr. Hensley disagreed that a problem existed. As a result, he refused to refund your money or exchange the MP3 player. You are unhappy with the MP3 player and your problem has not been settled. You have decided to file a complaint with the local Better Business Bureau.

Better Business Bureau of Chicago and Northern Illinois
Chicago, Illinois 60611

COMPLAINT FORM

PLEASE FOLLOW ENCLOSED INSTRUCTIONS

Date of Transaction _2/10/xx_   Date You Complained to Company _2/10/xx_   To Whom _Mike Hensley_

Sales Person _____   Identify Product/Service _MP3_   If Advertised, When _2/8/xx_

Where (Enclose Ad) _Local Newspaper_   Receipt, Contract, or Policy Number _____

COMPANY _Super Items_   YOUR NAME _(Student response.)_

ADDRESS _111 South Adams Street_   ADDRESS _(Student response.)_

CITY _Anytown, IL 33614_   CITY _(Student response.)_
        State   Zip Code   State   Zip Code

YOUR EMPLOYER'S FIRM NAME: _(Student response.)_   YOUR DAYTIME PHONE NO. _(Student response.)_

BRIEFLY EXPLAIN YOUR COMPLAINT AND FOLLOW THE ENCLOSED INSTRUCTIONS:

(Sample response.) The MP3 player was advertised as "easy to operate" with "satisfaction guaranteed." I found the player difficult to operate, but the store manager, Mr. Hensley, refused to give me a refund or exchange. I do not feel this is "satisfaction guaranteed."

_____

_____

_____

_____

_____

_____

What Adjustment Do You Consider Mutually Fair? _(Sample response.) the return of the MP3 player for a refund or exchange for a different player of equal value_

Your Signature   Date

Avoiding Consumer Fraud

Activity J	Name_____
Chapter 24	Date_____Period_____

Read the cases below and determine whether they are legitimate consumer contacts or examples of phishing or vishing. Explain your answers.

1. Jennifer has a Suncoast credit card. Their official Web site is www.suncoast.com. Jennifer received an e-mail from Suncoast credit cards with the following message:

   Save up to hundreds of dollars by transferring your high-interest balances to your Suncoast credit card. Use our *savings calculator* to determine how much money you can save. Act quickly because this offer expires April 30, 20xx. *Click here* to learn more. *Click here to transfer balances now*. (The hyperlinks open www.suncoast.com.)

   Legitimate—Companies such as Suncoast often use e-mail to market offers to existing customers, but they

   do not ask for personal information. Legitimate e-mails link to the real company's Web address—in this

   case, Suncoast.com.

2. Patrick has an internet account with Quicknet. Their official Web site is www.quicknet.com. He received the following e-mail from Quicknet-Database using the address information-quicknet@billing.org.

   As a valued Quicknet customer, this e-mail is being sent to inform you that your Quicknet account information has expired. Unless you update your account information immediately, we will be forced to block access to your account. To update your account *click here* (www.quicknet-reactivation.net).

   Phishing—The URL link in the e-mail does not link to www.quicknet.com, the official domain. Phishing

   e-mails often use false domains (such as www.quicknet-reactivation.net) that contain some of the real

   company's name.

3. Lorena received a telephone call from a person claiming to be a customer service representative from First Bank. The representative tells Lorena there is a problem with her account and gives her a toll free number to call to straighten out the problem.

   Vishing—Since Lorena was asked to call a toll free number, any information she provides may be used

   illegally.

4. Jestina received a telephone call from a person claiming to be a customer service representative from Holland National Bank. The representative explains that they have received a request for payment from Martin's Jewelry Store for $516.45 for a bracelet purchased on March 3, 20xx. The representative is calling to verify that Jestina made this purchase. He does not ask for her account number or other personal or financial information.

   Legitimate—Jestina was asked only to verify a purchase. She was not asked for any personal or financial

   information.

25 Using Credit

Understanding Credit

Activity A

Chapter 25

Name _____

Date _____ Period _____

Complete the following exercise to check your knowledge of credit.

1. Define *credit*. _the present use of future income that allows consumers to buy goods and services now and_ _pay for them later_

2. Explain how to determine your debt-to-income ratio. _total all monthly debts and divide that amount_ _by monthly take home pay_

3. What does it mean to establish credit? _to build a credit history as a person who is likely to repay debt_

4. Why is it important to establish good credit? _Creditors want evidence that any money loaned to a_ _person will be repaid._

5. What is a credit rating? _the creditor's evaluation of a person's willingness and ability to pay debts_

6. What does it mean when a person is called a good credit risk? _It means the person can be trusted to pay_ _their debts._

7. What traits do creditors consider when deciding if you are a good credit risk? _have a steady income;_ _make regular, on-time payments; own a car, home, stocks, or bonds; live in the same community for a_ _period of time_

8. List the advantages of using credit. _allows you to buy and use expensive goods and services as you pay_ _for them; convenience; source of cash for emergency or unexpected expenses_

9. List the disadvantages of using credit. _expensive; may spend more money than you have; may encourage_ _impulse purchases_

(Continued)

Name_____

10. Name the six types of credit available to consumers. credit card accounts, charge accounts, installment accounts, vehicle leasing, cash loans, home equity loans

11. Explain how a revolving charge account works. Customers have the choice of paying for purchases in full each month or spreading payments over a period of time.

12. What is the difference between a charge account and an installment account? In a charge account, the business bills the customer once a month, and the customer is expected to pay in full by the assigned due date. In an installment account, the buyer pays for the merchandise according to a set schedule of payments.

13. Why must a borrower pledge something of value as collateral to get a cash loan? If you are unable to repay the loan, the collateral serves as repayment.

14. What are the first steps you could take to establish credit? Get a job and stay employed. Open a checking account. Open a savings account. Buy an item on a layaway plan. Apply to a gasoline company or a local store for a credit card.

15. What information is included in a credit record? personal identification information; public record information; collection agency account information; credit account information; companies that requested your credit file

16. What is the purpose of a credit bureau? to collect and keep files of financial information on individual consumers

17. Why is it important to carefully examine a credit agreement before you sign it? It is a legally binding contract.

18. What should you do if you have a problem getting credit? Check your credit report for errors or missing information.

19. If you ever have a problem paying your bills on time, what should you do about your creditors? Notify creditors promptly and try to work out a temporary payment schedule.

20. What should you do if your credit card is lost or stolen? Report the loss or theft immediately.

Applying for Credit

Activity B

Chapter 25

Name _____

Date _____ Period _____

Complete the following credit application form. Then answer the questions that follow.
(Sample responses are shown.)

SEARS, ROEBUCK AND CO. INDIVIDUAL CREDIT ACCOUNT APPLICANT

APPLICATION TO BE COMPLETED IN NAME OF PERSON IN WHICH THE ACCOUNT IS TO BE CARRIED.

COURTESY TITLES ARE OPTIONAL   PLEASE PRINT

☐ MR. ☐ MRS. ☐ MISS ☒ MS. Jennifer (First Name) A. (Initial) Cook (Last Name)

4080 Tates Creek Rd. (Street Address) Lexington (City) KY (State) 40517 (Zip Code)

Phone No: Home 866-401-1001 Phone No: Business 866-414-7862 Soc. Sec. No. 321-55-1076 Age 20 Number of Dependents (Excluding Applicant) 0

Are you a United States citizen? ☒ Yes ☐ No If NO, explain immigration status: N/A

How Long at Present Address 3 yrs. Own ☐ Rent-Furnished ☐ Rent-Unfurnished ☒ Board ☐ Monthly Rent or Mortgage Payments $ 750

Name of Landlord John Ross Street Address 210 S. Henry St. City and State Lexington, KY

Former Address (if less than 2 years at present address) N/A How long N/A

Employer Stevenson Law Offices Street Address 3620 Park Place City and State Lexington, KY

How long 2 yrs. Occupation Receptionist Net Income $ 390 Monthly ☐ Weekly ☒

Former Employer (If less than 1 year with present employer) N/A How long

> ALIMONY, CHILD SUPPORT, OR SEPARATE MAINTENANCE INCOME NEED NOT BE REVEALED IF YOU DO NOT WISH TO HAVE IT CONSIDERED AS A BASIS FOR PAYING THIS OBLIGATION.

Alimony, child support, separate maintenance received under: N/A

☐ Court order ☐ Written agreement ☐ Oral understanding Amount $ _____

Other income, if any: Amount $ _____ Source _____

Name and Address of Bank First Bank, 620 Lafayette Savings ☒ Acc't No. 787 254 7 Checking ☒ Acc't No. 760 212 8 Loan ☐ Acc't No. _____

Previous Sears Account ☐ Yes ☒ No N/A (At What Sears Store) Account No. Is Account ☐ Yes Paid in Full ☐ No Date Final Payment Made _____

Relative or Personal Reference Other than Spouse Robert Cook (Name) 9176 Romany Rd. (Street Address) Lexington, KY (City and State) Father (Relationship)

(Continued)

Name_____

CREDIT REFERENCES
Attach additional sheet if necessary

List all references
(Open or closed within past two years)

Charge Accounts Loan References Store/Company Address	Date Opened	Name Account Carried in	Account Number	Balance	Monthly Payments
N/A					

Authorized buyer _____ N/A _____

| First Name | Initial | Last Name | Relationship to applicant |

Authorized buyer _____ N/A _____

| First Name | Initial | Last Name | Relationship to applicant |

SEARS IS AUTHORIZED TO INVESTIGATE MY CREDIT RECORD AND TO VERIFY MY CREDIT, EMPLOYMENT AND INCOME REFERENCES.

SIGNATURE OF APPLICANT X *Jennifer A. Cook* _____ DATE _05/29/XX_

THE INFORMATION BELOW IS REQUIRED IF: (1) YOUR SPOUSE IS AN AUTHORIZED BUYER OR (2) YOU RESIDE IN A COMMUNITY PROPERTY STATE (ARIZONA, CALIFORNIA, IDAHO, LOUISIANA, NEVADA, NEW MEXICO, TEXAS, WASHINGTON) OR (3) YOU ARE RELYING ON THE INCOME OR ASSETS OF ANOTHER PERSON, INCLUDING A SPOUSE OR FORMER SPOUSE, AS A BASIS FOR PAYMENT.

Name of spouse ☐
Name of former spouse ☐ N/A
Name of other person ☐ _____

| | Street Address | Address | City and State | Age |

Employer _____

How long _____ Occupation _____ Soc. Sec. No. _____ Net Income $ _____ Monthly ☐ Weekly ☐

Savings ☐ Acc't No. _____
Checking ☐ Acc't No. _____
Name and Address of Bank _____ Loan ☐ Acc't No. _____

THE PERSON ON WHOSE INCOME OR ASSETS YOU ARE RELYING AS A BASIS FOR PAYMENT MUST SIGN BELOW. HOWEVER, YOUR SPOUSE NEED NOT SIGN IF YOU RESIDE IN A COMMUNITY PROPERTY STATE OR IF YOUR SPOUSE IS AN AUTHORIZED BUYER.

SEARS IS AUTHORIZED TO INVESTIGATE MY CREDIT RECORD AND TO VERIFY MY CREDIT, EMPLOYMENT AND INCOME REFERENCES.

X _____
(Signature of person on whose income or assets applicant is relying.)   Date _____

Based on the information you have given in this application, would you consider yourself to be a good credit risk? Explain. __Yes. I have consistently held a job for 2 years. I make a monthly rent payment. I have a__ __checking and savings account.__

_____

_____

_____

_____

What steps could you take to build a good credit rating? Explain. __continue with current employment; follow__ __guidelines of savings and checking accounts; buy items on layaway; obtain a store or gasoline credit card; pay__ __bills on time__

_____

_____

_____

_____

Cost of Credit

Activity C

Chapter 25

Name_____

Date_____Period_____

Read the following story about Nancy. Then answer the questions that follow.

Case Study: Nancy decided to purchase a new television on credit. The selling price of the television is $650.00. The salesperson told Nancy the store would finance the television for one year at an annual percentage rate of 15 percent or for two years at a rate of 12 percent. Nancy must decide which option to take.

1. Define *finance charge*. the total amount a borrower must pay for the use of credit _____

_____

2. How much interest will Nancy pay if she finances the television for one year? $97.50 _____

3. How much interest will Nancy pay if she finances the television for two years? $156 _____

4. What is the total cost of the television if she finances it for one year? $747.50 _____

5. What is the total cost of the television if she finances it for two years? $806 _____

6. By law, what are creditors required to tell Nancy concerning her finance charges? The finance charge

must be stated as a dollar amount and as an annual percentage rate. _____

7. Would you advise Nancy to finance the television for one year or for two years? Explain. _____

(Sample response.) One year. Nancy would be paying more in interest with the two-year plan. However, if

she chose the two-year plan and paid the purchase off early, she would benefit more from the lower interest

rate of 12%. _____

_____

_____

_____

_____

8. Do you think the television is worth the price Nancy must pay? Why? (Sample response.) No. At a

minimum, Nancy would have to pay an additional $97.50 for the television because of the 15% interest.

Nancy might be able to find a better deal elsewhere. _____

_____

9. How else might Nancy purchase the television? (Sample response.) She could pay cash, pay cash with

money from her savings account, or save her money and buy the television later. _____

_____

_____

Federal Credit Laws

Activity D

Chapter 25

Name _____

Date _____ Period _____

Six federal credit laws are listed below. Match each law to its description(s). (The laws may be used more than once.)

A. Truth in Lending Act
B. Fair Credit Reporting Act
C. Equal Credit Opportunity Act
D. Fair Credit Billing Act
E. Electronic Funds Transfer Act
F. Fair Debt Collection Practices Act

_____C_____ 1. Prohibits a creditor from denying credit on the basis of sex, marital status, race, religion, age, or for receiving public assistance.

_____D_____ 2. Requires creditors to send customers a written explanation of steps to take when a billing error or question occurs.

_____A_____ 3. Requires creditors to tell customers the cost of credit before they use it.

_____E_____ 4. Can limit your liability if you report a lost or stolen credit card promptly.

_____B_____ 5. Provides for confidentiality of information contained in credit reports.

_____D_____ 6. Protects consumers against unfair billing.

_____A_____ 7. Limits a cardholder's liability to $50 if a lost or stolen credit card is used by someone else.

_____B_____ 8. Provides for accuracy of information contained in credit reports.

_____A_____ 9. Prohibits businesses from issuing or mailing credit cards to people who have not requested them.

_____F_____ 10. Protects consumers from abusive, unfair, or deceptive conduct by collection agencies.

_____E_____ 11. Applies to the use of computers, ATMs, debit cards, and other electronic banking transactions.

_____F_____ 12. Prohibits collection agencies from revealing or publicizing a debtor's debt to other people.

_____E_____ 13. Limits loss to $50 if you notify the institution within two days of a lost or stolen credit card.

Using Credit Wisely

Activity E

Chapter 25

Name_____

Date_____Period_____

Identify an item you would like to buy on credit. Contact three creditors and compare the credit terms available from them to allow you to purchase the item. Then answer the following questions about using credit wisely.

Item _(Student response.)_ _____

Creditor 1. Name of Business: _(Student response.)_ _____

1. What is the size of the loan? _(Student response.)_ _____

2. What is the APR for the loan? _(Student response.)_ _____

3. What is the repayment time? _(Student response.)_ _____

4. What is the total cost of the loan plus the interest? _(Student response.)_ _____

Creditor 2. Name of Business: _(Student response.)_ _____

1. What is the size of the loan? _(Student response.)_ _____

2. What is the APR for the loan? _(Student response.)_ _____

3. What is the repayment time? _(Student response.)_ _____

4. What is the total cost of the loan plus the interest? _(Student response.)_ _____

Creditor 3. Name of Business: _(Student response.)_ _____

1. What is the size of the loan? _(Student response.)_ _____

2. What is the APR for the loan? _(Student response.)_ _____

3. What is the repayment time? _(Student response.)_ _____

4. What is the total cost of the loan plus the interest? _(Student response.)_ _____

---

1. Based on your comparison, would you purchase the item on credit? Why or why not? _____

   (Student response.) _____

   _____

2. From which creditor would you purchase the item? _(Student response.)_ _____

   Why? _(Student response.)_ _____

   _____

   _____

   _____

(Continued)

Name_____

3. If you do not purchase the item on credit, how could you pay for it? *(Sample response.)*
   Save money and pay cash.
   _____

4. What are some signs of credit problems? *(See 25-11 on page 540 of the text.)*
   _____
   _____
   _____

5. If you lose control of your credit and cannot afford to make your payments, what should you do? _____
   Notify your creditors immediately and set up a repayment schedule to reduce the size of monthly
   payments.

6. How can credit counseling help you with credit problems? Credit counseling helps debtors work out
   financial programs to repay debts, learn to manage money to prevent future debt, and work out repayment
   schedules with creditors.
   _____

7. What is bankruptcy? a legal proceeding for the purpose of stating a person's inability to pay debts
   _____
   _____
   _____

8. What is the difference between Chapter 7 bankruptcy and Chapter 13 bankruptcy? In Chapter 7
   bankruptcy, a person's assets, including car, house, and furniture, are sold by the court to pay the debts. In
   Chapter 13 bankruptcy, debtors pay back some or most of their debts over a three- to five-year period and
   keep all their possessions.
   _____

9. If you purchase an item under a finance plan that offers "no finance charges for six months," what
   happens when you have not paid off the loan in full in the seventh month? You must pay interest on the
   amount from the purchase date.
   _____
   _____

10. What steps could you take to assure that you do not have finance charges when you purchase an item
    under the terms "no finance charges for six months"? Budget monthly payments so the amount is paid
    in full before the expiration date.
    _____
    _____

Banking, Saving, and Investing

Compare Financial Institutions

Name_____

Date_____Period_____

Working in groups, survey three local financial institutions about the services they offer by finding out the information below. Decide on one type of banking account to compare at these financial institutions. Complete the questions that follow. Make a presentation to the class about your research. (Chart answers are student response.)

Type of account: _____

	Minimum Balance	**Age Requirement**	**Charges**	**Interest Rates**
Institution 1 (name):				
Institution 2 (name):				
Institution 3 (name):				

1. What other types of accounts are offered by the above financial institutions? __(Student response.)__

_____

_____

_____

(Continued)

Name_____

2. Are any special services available to customers at these financial institutions?

Institution 1: _(Student response.)_____

_____

Institution 2: _(Student response.)_____

_____

Institution 3: _(Student response.)_____

_____

3. What are the policies and charges for using automatic teller machines (ATMs)?

Institution 1: _(Student response.)_____

_____

Institution 2: _(Student response.)_____

_____

Institution 3: _(Student response.)_____

_____

4. Why is it important to know the insurance policies the financial institutions have? _so you can be sure_

_your money is safe_____

_____

5. Which institution did your team prefer? Explain. _(Student response.)_____

_____

_____

_____

_____

_____

_____

_____

_____

_____

6. How can choosing the right financial institution help you manage money effectively? _____

(Sample response.) Looking at the financial institution's convenience and costs of the services you need can

help you manage money more effectively.

7. What conveniences has online banking provided for consumers? _(Answers may vary.) finances can be_

managed through your computer; transactions can take place at any time of the day or night; bills can be

paid online

Checks

Activity B

Chapter 26

Name _____

Date _____ Period _____

Every number and word on a check is important. Identify the information on the checks below in the spaces provided.

A bank's name/address

B account holder's name/address

C bank's identification number

D check number

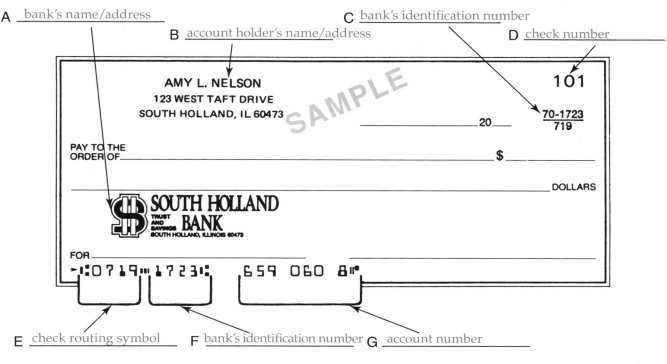

E check routing symbol

F bank's identification number

G account number

H payee's name

I date

J check amount in numbers

K check purpose

L check amount in words

M signature

Using a Checking Account

Activity C

Chapter 26

Name_____

Date_____Period_____

Terry Johnson has a checking account at South Holland Trust and Savings Bank. Assume you are Terry Johnson and complete the following banking transactions.

Making a Deposit

You want to deposit $43.00 in currency, $2.78 in coins, a check in the amount of $28.55, and a check in the amount of $98.29. Using this information and today's date, fill out this deposit slip.

```
DEPOSIT TICKET

TERRY JOHNSON
123 W. TAFT DRIVE
SOUTH HOLLAND, IL   60473

DATE August 10              20 XX

Terry Johnson

SOUTH HOLLAND
TRUST AND SAVINGS BANK  SOUTH HOLLAND, ILL. 60473
```

CASH	CURRENCY	43	00
	COIN	2	78
LIST CHECKS SINGLY		28	55
		98	29
TOTAL FROM OTHER SIDE			
TOTAL		172	62
LESS CASH RECEIVED			
NET DEPOSIT		172	62

70-1723/719

USE OTHER SIDE FOR ADDITIONAL LISTING

BE SURE EACH ITEM IS PROPERLY ENDORSED

⑆⑉071917232⑉ ⑆616⑈765⑈6⑈

CHECKS AND OTHER ITEMS ARE RECEIVED FOR DEPOSIT SUBJECT TO THE PROVISIONS OF THE UNIFORM COMMERCIAL CODE OR ANY APPLICABLE COLLECTION AGREEMENT.

Writing a Check

Write a check for $35.24 to pay for books purchased at Webster's Bookstore. Use today's date.

```
TERRY JOHNSON                                              237
123 W. TAFT DRIVE
SOUTH HOLLAND, IL   60473   SAMPLE   August 12  20 XX   70-1723/719

PAY TO THE
ORDER OF  Webster's Bookstore                        $ 35.24

thirty-five and 24/100 _____ DOLLARS

SOUTH HOLLAND
TRUST AND SAVINGS BANK  SOUTH HOLLAND, ILL. 60473

MEMO books                          Terry Johnson

⑆⑉071917232⑉  ⑆616⑈765⑈6⑈
```

(Continued)

Name_____

Filling Out a Check Register

Record the amounts of your deposit and the check to Webster's Bookstore in this register. Your previous balance was $185.64.

NUMBER	DATE	DESCRIPTION OF TRANSACTION	PAYMENT/DEBIT (−)		✓ T	FEE (IF ANY) (−)	DEPOSIT/CREDIT (+)	BALANCE $
		RECORD ALL CHARGES OR CREDITS THAT AFFECT YOUR ACCOUNT						185 64
—	8/10	deposit	$			$	$ 172 62	172 62
								358 26
237	8/12	Webster's Bookstore	35 24					35 24
		books						323 02

Balancing a Bank Statement

Your bank statement shows a closing balance of $299.67. Both the deposit you made earlier and the check you wrote in this activity are not shown on the statement. Also, you have five additional outstanding checks: $13.37 (#228), $51.30 (#230), $7.32 (#231), $25.00 (#232), and $17.04 (#235). Use this information to fill in this worksheet. The balance on the worksheet should be the same as the balance above in the check register.

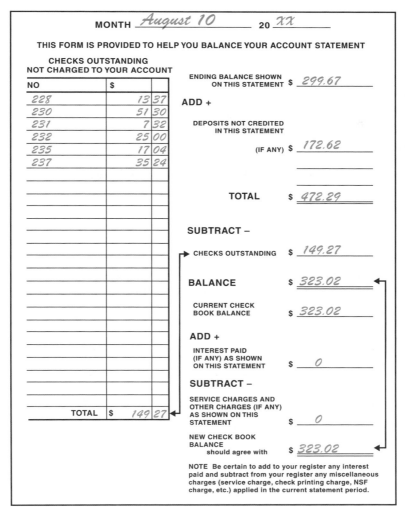

MONTH _August 10_ 20 _XX_

THIS FORM IS PROVIDED TO HELP YOU BALANCE YOUR ACCOUNT STATEMENT

CHECKS OUTSTANDING
NOT CHARGED TO YOUR ACCOUNT

NO	$
228	13 37
230	51 30
231	7 32
232	25 00
235	17 04
237	35 24
TOTAL	$ 149 27

ENDING BALANCE SHOWN ON THIS STATEMENT $ _299.67_

ADD +

DEPOSITS NOT CREDITED IN THIS STATEMENT

(IF ANY) $ _172.62_

TOTAL $ _472.29_

SUBTRACT −

CHECKS OUTSTANDING $ _149.27_

BALANCE $ _323.02_

CURRENT CHECK BOOK BALANCE $ _323.02_

ADD +

INTEREST PAID (IF ANY) AS SHOWN ON THIS STATEMENT $ _0_

SUBTRACT −

SERVICE CHARGES AND OTHER CHARGES (IF ANY) AS SHOWN ON THIS STATEMENT $ _0_

NEW CHECK BOOK BALANCE should agree with $ _323.02_

NOTE Be certain to add to your register any interest paid and subtract from your register any miscellaneous charges (service charge, check printing charge, NSF charge, etc.) applied in the current statement period.

Safe-Deposit Boxes

Activity D   Name _____

Chapter 26   Date _____ Period _____

In the list of items below, check those that should be stored in a safe-deposit box. Then answer the questions that follow.

____✓____ 1. Birth certificate

_____ 2. Checkbook

_____ 3. Driver's license

____✓____ 4. Will

____✓____ 5. Title of car ownership

_____ 6. Check stubs

____✓____ 7. Precious jewelry

____✓____ 8. Deeds to property

_____ 9. Credit cards

____✓____ 10. Stocks

_____ 11. Bank statements

____✓____ 12. Bonds

____✓____ 13. Insurance policies

____✓____ 14. Old gold coins

_____ 15. Social security card

16. What is the purpose of using a safe-deposit box? _to protect and safely store your valuables from fire_
      and theft _____

      _____

      _____

17. What are the policies (rates, hours of accessibility, security measures, etc.) for using a safe-deposit box at a financial institution in your community? Name the institution and describe the policies. _____
      (Student response.) _____

      _____

      _____

      _____

      _____

      _____

      _____

Investing Your Money

Activity E

Chapter 26

Name _____

Date _____ Period _____

Read the statements below and write the missing terms in the crossword puzzle.

Across

2. Stocks, bonds, and mutual funds.
4. Bonds issued by a corporation. (two words)
7. A tax-deferred retirement savings plan.
8. Bonds that are more a source of savings than an investment. (two words)
10. Certificates of debt or obligation issued by a corporation or government.
11. An investment in land or building property. (two words)
12. Investments in a variety of securities such as preferred stock, common stock, and bonds. (two words)

Down

1. Bonds issued by state, county, or city government. (two words)
2. A share of ownership in a corporation.
3. A company that collects money from a number of investors and invests that money in securities. (two words)
5. A type of stock that is a more conservative investment and involves less risk. (two words)
6. A type of stock that involves more risk. (two words)
9. A tax-deferred retirement plan for self-employed people or employees of unincorporated companies that do not have their own pension plan.

Banking and Investment Terms

Activity F
Chapter 26

Name _____
Date _____ Period _____

Complete the following statements by filling in the blanks.

Commercial — 1. _____ banks are often called full-service banks because of their many services.

FDIC — 2. In most commercial banks and savings banks, the money you deposit is safe because it is insured by the _____ for up to $100,000.

bank — 3. A savings _____ offers many of the same services provided by commercial banks.

credit union — 4. A(n) _____ _____ differs from a commercial bank and a savings bank in that its services are for its members only.

NCUA — 5. Most credit unions are insured by the _____.

electronic funds transfer — 6. A(n) _____ _____ _____ authorizes your bank to electronically pay certain bills directly from your account each month.

automated teller machine — 7. A(n) _____ _____ _____ can be used to withdraw money from your account when you are shopping in the mall.

PIN — 8. In order to use an ATM, you must have a(n) _____.

debit card — 9. You may pay for purchases in a store without cash, check, or credit cards by using a(n) _____ _____.

Express — 10. _____ checking works very well for people who use online banking, banking by phone, or ATMs to do all their banking.

NOW account — 11. A(n) _____ _____ is good to have if you want an interest-bearing account and can maintain the minimum balance.

interest-bearing — 12. A(n) _____-_____ checking account allows you to earn interest and write checks on the same account.

joint — 13. When two or more people share a bank account, it is called a(n) _____ account.

blank — 14. A check with a(n) _____ endorsement can be cashed by anyone who possesses it.

restrictive — 15. *For deposit only* is a common _____ check endorsement.

bank statement — 16. A(n) _____ _____ is a record of the checks, deposits, and charges made to your account for a specific length of time.

traveler's — 17. If you are going to be traveling, _____ checks are convenient to use.

cashier's — 18. If you are paying a large sum of money, a(n) _____ check may be a more acceptable form of payment than a personal check.

certified — 19. A(n) _____ check is a personal check with a bank's guarantee that the check will be paid.

money order — 20. If you do not have a checking account, you can use a(n) _____ _____ to make a payment safely by mail.

Safe-deposit boxes — 21. _____-_____ _____ are small metal containers people rent to protect their valuables from fire and theft.

regular — 22. A(n) _____ savings account is a convenient form of savings, but it pays the lowest rate of interest.

certificate of deposit — 23. With a(n) _____ _____ _____, you deposit money for a set period of time and earn a set annual rate of interest.

Insurance

Auto Insurance

Read the following cases about auto insurance. Then answer the questions related to each case. Discuss the cases and answers in class.

Case 1: Kevin talked to his insurance agent about buying auto insurance. The agent gave several examples of the types of problems Kevin might have and how auto insurance could protect him. Indicate which type of auto insurance would cover each possible problem.

A. bodily injury liability

B. property damage liability

C. medical payments

D. uninsured/underinsured motorists

E. comprehensive

F. collision

___B___ 1. During a rainstorm, Kevin swerves to miss a dog, runs into a fence, and damages it.

___E___ 2. A compact disc, books, and tools are stolen from Kevin's car.

___D___ 3. As Kevin drives his friend Juan to school, another driver runs a stop sign and hits Kevin's car. Both Kevin and Juan are injured. The driver of the other car does not have insurance.

___F___ 4. Kevin runs into a telephone pole, causing $700 worth of damage to the front of his car.

___A___ 5. Coming home from a party, Kevin daydreams and runs into another car. The people in that car are injured.

___C___ 6. Kevin is injured in a car accident.

Case 2: When Latrice bought her car from a used car dealer, he suggested a local insurance company to her. She took his advice and bought insurance with the company. She thought the premiums seemed high for the amount of coverage she would receive, but she did not want to take the time to talk to other companies. Latrice's father was angry when she told him about the insurance she had purchased. "Why did you not shop around? Why did you not compare premiums and coverages?" he asked.

1. What factors determine Latrice's insurance premium rate? (Answers may vary.) age, driving record, year and model of car, where you live, distance you drive, amount of deductible, completion of a driver education or safety course

2. What are some questions Latrice should ask the next time she shops for insurance? (Sample response.) What discounts can I receive? What is the deductible? What is included in the coverage?

3. Why is it important to shop around and compare premiums and coverages? (Sample response.) to obtain all of the coverage you may need at an affordable price

(Continued)

Name_____

Case 3: John plans to buy an old used pick-up truck. Although the truck runs fairly well, the body is in bad shape. John says, "I will only carry collision insurance. I do not need bodily injury or property damage liability coverage."

1. Was John right in his decision? Explain. (Sample response.) No. Most states have financial responsibility laws, which require you to have bodily injury liability and property damage liability insurance. If John is involved in an accident without liability insurance, he could have his driver's license or car registration suspended.

2. What advice would you give to John? (Sample response.) Due to the age of the vehicle, collision insurance may not be worthwhile. The vehicle may not be worth the costs of the premium and deductible. Obtain the bodily injury liability and property damage liability insurance needed based on state law.

Case 4: Julie plans to spend most of her money on a nice car. She says she will not have enough money left to buy insurance. "I will drive extra careful until I can afford to buy auto insurance," she says.

1. Can Julie drive a car without buying auto insurance? Explain. (Sample response.) No. Financial responsibility laws are designed to make sure that motorists can pay for any damages or injuries they may cause while driving their cars.

2. What problems could Julie have because she does not have auto insurance? (Sample response.) If Julie could not show proof of liability insurance, she could have her license or car registration suspended. Julie could also become involved in an accident resulting in large expenses, which she would not be able to afford.

3. What is the best thing for Julie to do until she can afford auto insurance? (Sample response.) Julie could consider purchasing a car that is not as expensive so she could afford insurance. She can continue to save her money until she can afford the more expensive car with the necessary insurance.

Case 5: Maurice is involved in an automobile accident with his friend William. Both are players on the school's basketball team, on their way to a championship game. They decide to get to the game on time and handle details about the accident later.

1. What advice would you give to Maurice and William? (Sample response.) Whenever you become involved in an accident, you should stay at the scene of the accident until police arrive. Do not discuss the accident with anyone other than the police or an insurance representative. Exchange information with the other driver. Notify the insurance company as soon as possible. Promptly notify the state's motor vehicle department or similar authority, as required by law.

What Do You Do If You Are in an Accident?

Activity B
Chapter 27

Name_____

Date_____ **Period**_____

If you are involved in an automobile accident, certain procedures need to be followed. Explain them below.

1. When involved in a car accident, you should: STOP immediately. Do not leave the scene of the accident. Notify the police immediately. Do not move the vehicle(s) until the police have arrived. Do not admit fault. You may be entirely blameless, but witnesses will help prove it. Avoid discussing the accident with anyone except the police or an identified representative of your insurance company. Exchange information with the other driver. Write down the other driver's name, address, telephone number, car license number, driver's license number, and insurance carrier; names and addresses of all witnesses; names and addresses of any injured persons; names and addresses of any passengers. Notify your insurance agent or insurance company as soon as possible. Promptly notify the state's motor vehicle department or similar authority, as required by law.

2. In some states, drivers are required by law to show proof of liability insurance if they are involved in an accident. Does your state require the proof of liability insurance coverage to be in the vehicle at all times? (Student response.)

3. What type of auto liability insurance coverage is required in your state? (Student response.)

4. If your state law requires proof of liability insurance coverage, what may happen to you if you do not have this proof of coverage? (Student response.)

Health Insurance

Activity C

Chapter 27

Name _____

Date _____ Period _____

Review the statements below and answer the questions that follow.

1. Spencer's arm was broken during a soccer game. He was taken to the hospital emergency room where his arm was X-rayed and set. The expenses were covered by his basic medical insurance. What other expenses does this type of insurance cover? hospitalization, laboratory tests, medicine, and possibly some of the costs of doctor visits and surgical procedures

2. Mr. Conway had heart surgery, which involved very costly medical bills. Fortunately, the Conway family had major medical insurance coverage in addition to basic medical coverage. What are the advantages to this additional medical insurance? It pays the largest share of expenses resulting from a major illness or injury. It may also pay for additional services such as doctor visits, prescription medications, and preventative care. Individuals may be able to qualify for a health savings account.

3. Mrs. Ramos wants to be able to use any doctor or hospital she wants. What type of health care policy should she purchase? fee-for-service plan

4. Marty had a sore throat and fever for two days. His parents are enrolled in an HMO through their company insurance. Where should Marty go for medical treatment? primary care physician

How much can Marty expect to pay at the HMO facility? either no charge or a minimal fee

5. Tawanda has joined a PPO through her employer. What should she consider when choosing a doctor? She must use a doctor or a hospital from the approved PPO list or pay higher fees.

How are the fees for medical service determined? The fees charged for medical services, which are negotiated with the PPO by Tawanda's group or insurance carrier, are usually discounted 10 to 20 percent.

6. Nathaniel has a POS plan through his employer. How does a POS plan differ from an HMO plan? A POS member may choose an HMO or PPO each time they seek medical services, but an HMO member cannot.

How will this affect Nathaniel's benefits? The cost of services will be higher if a primary physician from the preferred list is not chosen.

7. What types of health insurance do you feel you should have? Explain. (Student response.)

Home Insurance Possessions Inventory

Activity D

Chapter 27

Name_____

Date_____Period_____

For home insurance purposes, prepare an inventory of your household possessions and estimate their values. Include the model or serial number and brand name whenever possible. Then answer the questions that follow. (Inventory is student response.)

Inventory	
Item	**Estimated Value**

1. What is the difference between homeowner's insurance and renter's insurance? _Homeowner's_ insurance provides coverage for property dwelling and possessions as well as liability if someone is injured on your property. Renter's insurance only covers your personal possessions.

2. Approximately how much home insurance coverage would you need to insure your possessions? _____ (Student response.)

3. What would be the advantage of having a large deductible? _A large deductible can help reduce_ premiums.

Insurance Terms to Know

Activity E **Name**____________________________________

Chapter 27 **Date**______________ **Period**__________________

Read the statements on the next page and write the missing terms in the crossword puzzle.

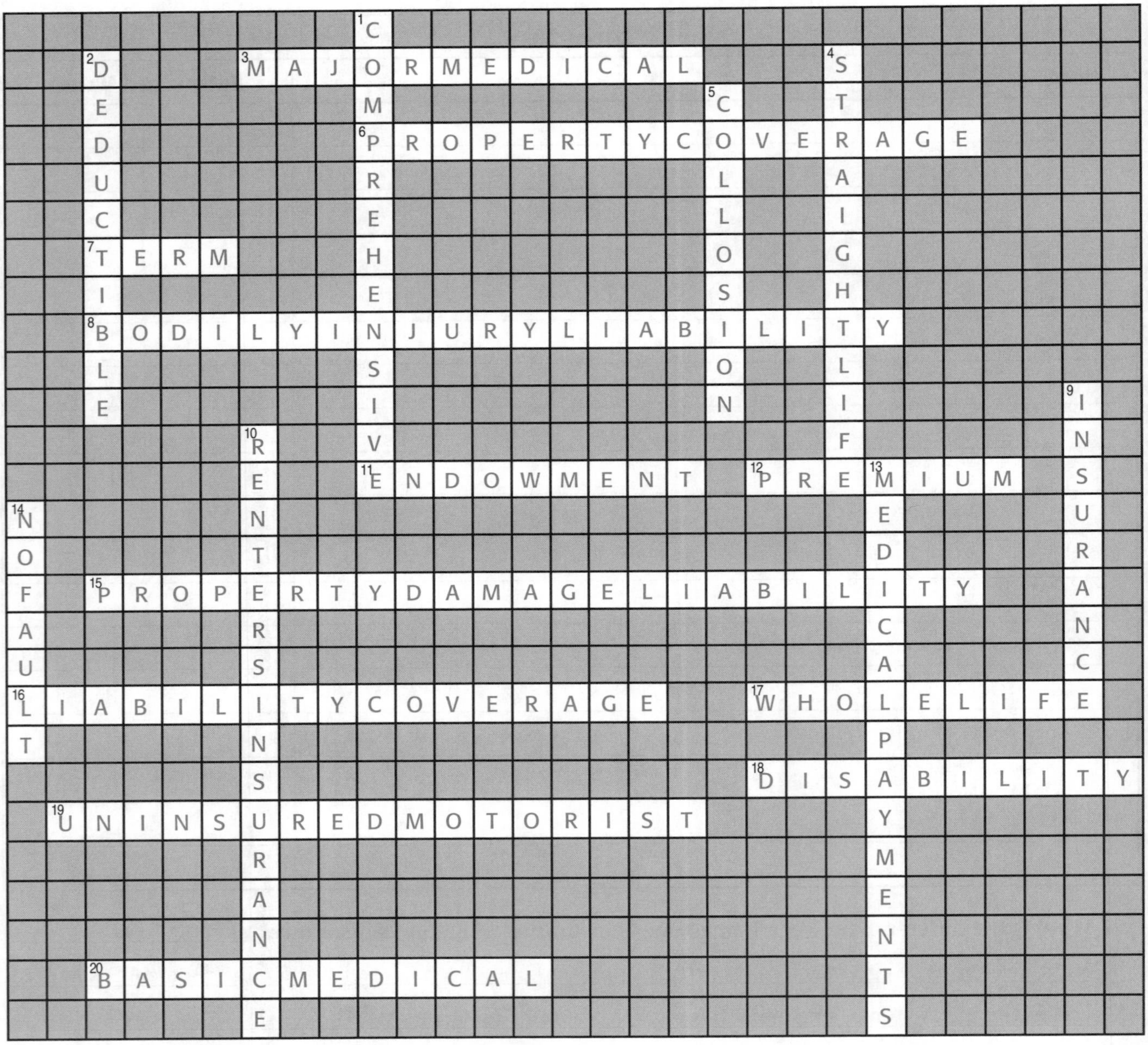
1 COMPREHENSIVE
2 DEDUCTIBLE
3 MAJORMEDICAL
4 STRAIGHTLIFE
5 COLLISION
6 PROPERTYCOVERAGE
7 TERM
8 BODILYINJURYLIABILITY
9 INSURANCE
10 RENTERSINSURANCE
11 ENDOWMENT
12 PREMIUM
13 MEDICALPAYMENTS
14 NOFAULT
15 PROPERTYDAMAGELIABILITY
16 LIABILITYCOVERAGE
17 WHOLELIFE
18 DISABILITY
19 UNINSUREDMOTORIST
20 BASICMEDICAL

(Continued)

Name_____

Across

3. Health insurance that pays the largest share of expenses resulting from a major illness or serious injury. (two words)
6. This type of home insurance coverage insures you against such damages as fire and lightning, burglary and theft, vandalism, and explosions. (two words)
7. This life insurance covers the policyholder for a set period of time specified in the policy.
8. Auto insurance coverage that protects you if you are legally liable for an accident in which others are injured or killed. (three words)
11. A form of whole life insurance in which payments are limited to a set period of time.
12. A set amount of money paid to an insurance company on a regular basis in return for financial protection in the event a misfortune occurs that is covered by the policy.
15. Auto insurance coverage that pays for damages your car causes to the property of others if you are responsible for an accident. (three words)
16. This type of home insurance coverage protects you against financial loss if others are injured on or by your property, or if you or your property accidentally damages the property of others. (two words)
17. This life insurance covers the policyholder for a lifetime. (two words)
18. A type of health insurance that provides regular income payments when a person is unable to work for an extended period of time because of injury or illness.
19. Auto insurance coverage that pays for bodily injuries for which a hit-and-run driver is responsible. (two words)
20. Health insurance that covers the costs of hospitalization. (two words)

Down

1. Auto insurance coverage that pays for damage to your car caused by something other than another vehicle.
2. The amount you must pay before the insurance company will pay a claim.
4. A policyholder pays premiums throughout his or her life with this type of whole life policy. (two words)
5. Auto insurance coverage that pays for the damage to your car caused by a collision with another vehicle or object.
9. A plan to help people protect themselves from unexpected financial losses.
10. This property protection only covers damage or loss of personal property and possessions, not the dwelling itself. (two words)
13. Auto insurance coverage that pays for the medical expenses resulting from an accident regardless of who was at fault. (two words)
14. Auto insurance protection designed to eliminate the legal process of proving who is at fault in an accident. (two words)

Life Insurance

Activity F

Chapter 27

Name_____

Date_____Period_____

Indicate whether the statements are true or false by writing either *true* or *false* in the blanks. Then answer the following questions.

false	1. If you have no dependents, you really need life insurance.
true	2. When a life insurance policyholder dies, the insurance company pays the face value of the policy to the beneficiary.
false	3. Term insurance is a form of savings.
true	4. Whole life insurance covers the policyholder for a lifetime.
true	5. Premiums are higher on endowment policies because the cash value builds up faster.
true	6. Term insurance pays benefits only if the policyholder dies during the term of the policy.
false	7. Premiums for term insurance are higher than those for whole life insurance.
true	8. A renewable privilege allows the policyholder to review the policy at standard rates regardless of any changes in health.
false	9. Whole life insurance is simply for protection; it builds no cash value.
true	10. The beneficiary is the person named by the policyholder to receive the death benefit.
false	11. Universal life insurance does not allow flexibility in the premium payments.
true	12. When evaluating job offers, you need to consider the insurance programs the company offers.
false	13. The insurance company, agent, or policy you choose makes no difference in the coverage you receive or the premiums you pay.

14. What form of life insurance would you purchase if you supported a spouse? Explain. _____
   (Student response.) _____

   _____

15. What form of life insurance would you purchase if you had children? Explain. (Student response.) _____

   _____

   _____

16. What form of life insurance would you purchase if you had no dependents? Explain._____
   (Student response.) _____

   _____

17. What form of life insurance would you purchase if you supported elderly parents? Explain. _____
   (Student response.) _____

   _____

Managing Family, Work, and Citizenship Roles

Your Family Role

Activity A

Chapter 28

Name _____

Date _____ Period _____

Select someone in your class to interview. Ask the questions below about their family roles.

Name of Interviewee: (Student response.) _____

1. What is your current role in your family? (Student response.) _____

2. Have you had any other roles in the past? (Student response.) _____

3. What are your commitments to your family? (Student response.) _____

   _____

   _____

4. What household responsibilities do you handle as a family member? (Student response.) ____

   _____

   _____

5. How are the household chores assigned in your family? (Student response.) _____

   _____

6. Do you consider your household assignments fair? Explain. (Student response.) _____

   _____

   _____

7. How would you assign household chores fairly? (Student response.) _____

   _____

   _____

8. What leisure activities do you share with family members? (Student response.) _____

   _____

9. How do you balance the demands of family, school, and work? (Student response.) _____

   _____

   _____

10. How could you be more successful in handling your family roles? (Student response.) ____

    _____

Managing Your Time

Activity B

Chapter 28

Name_____

Date_____Period_____

In order to balance your family and work roles, you need to plan and use your time wisely. List below the tasks you need to complete today. Then rank the top 10 tasks in order of priority. As you complete each task on the list, place a check in the space provided. At the end of the day, evaluate your plan by answering the questions at the bottom of the page.   (Answers are student response.)

Tasks for the day: _____

_____

_____

To-Do List

Done

_____ 1. _____

_____ 2. _____

_____ 3. _____

_____ 4. _____

_____ 5. _____

_____ 6. _____

_____ 7. _____

_____ 8. _____

_____ 9. _____

_____ 10. _____

Did you waste any time? If so, how?_____

_____

How will you avoid time-wasters in the future?_____

_____

_____

During which tasks did you procrastinate?_____

_____

Were your deadlines realistic? Explain. _____

_____

_____

How did you stay motivated to complete the tasks? _____

_____

_____

Support Systems

Activity C	**Name**_____
Chapter 28	**Date**_____**Period**_____

Working with a partner, identify four support programs available in your community and describe them. Search the Internet, talk to friends and neighbors, read local newspapers, or contact local government offices to locate the groups that provide the programs. Report the results of your fact-finding below and be prepared to share your findings with the class.   (Answers are student response.)

Organization 1: _____

Name of program: _____

Target audience: _____

Program description: _____

_____

_____

_____

Organization 2: _____

Name of program: _____

Target audience: _____

Program description: _____

_____

_____

_____

Organization 3: _____

Name of program: _____

Target audience: _____

Program description: _____

_____

_____

_____

Organization 4: _____

Name of program: _____

Target audience: _____

Program description: _____

_____

_____

_____

Legal Terms

Activity D

Chapter 28

Name _____

Date _____ Period _____

Complete the following sentences by filling in the blank.

_____register_____   1. When you _____ to vote, you add your name to a list of people who are allowed to vote.

_____Public laws_____   2. _____ _____ govern the association between citizens and the government.

_____Civil laws_____   3. _____ _____ outline citizens' rights in relation to one another.

_____International laws_____   4. _____ _____ outline policies for dealing with foreign governments.

_____Administrative laws_____   5. _____ _____ relate to the duties and powers of presidents and governors.

_____criminal law_____   6. The purpose of _____ _____ is to protect society from offenses considered wrong and unjust.

_____Constitutional laws_____   7. _____ _____ establish the basic rights and freedoms of all citizens.

_____felony_____   8. Murder, rape, or kidnapping would be considered a(n) _____.

_____misdemeanor_____   9. Speeding or disorderly conduct would be considered a(n) _____.

_____contract_____   10. A legally binding agreement between two or more people is a(n) _____.

_____valid_____   11. In order for a contract to be _____, both parties must agree on the terms, be competent, be 18 years or older, and give consideration.

_____parties_____   12. Persons entering into a contract are called _____.

_____competent_____   13. A person who is able to understand the terms of a contract is considered _____.

_____Consideration_____   14. _____ means each party must give up something in order to receive what the other party is offering.

_____tort_____   15. A wrongful act committed against another person, independent of a contract, is a(n) _____.

Consulting a Lawyer

Activity E

Chapter 28

Name_____

Date_____Period_____

Answer the following questions about consulting a lawyer.

1. When you have an important financial or legal decision to make, when is the best time to consult a lawyer?

   before you make the decision or a serious problem arises

2. What are six examples of cases when a lawyer should be contacted? (Answers may vary.)

   A. buying or selling real estate

   B. writing or entering into a contract

   C. getting divorced

   D. experiencing financial problems

   E. writing a will

   F. being charged with a criminal action or facing a civil suit

3. How can you find a good lawyer? Ask a trusted teacher, friend, or family member to suggest a lawyer, or call the Lawyer Referral and Information Service (LRIS).

4. What is the Lawyer Referral and Information Service (LRIS) and how can you locate it? The Lawyer Referral and Information Service (LRIS) is a service sponsored by local bar associations whose phone number can usually be found in the Yellow Pages under Attorneys or Lawyers. You may also find a link through the American Bar Association Web site at www.abanet.org.

5. If you cannot afford to hire a lawyer, where might you find legal assistance for no or low cost?_____

   a legal aid office or a legal aid clinic at a law school

6. Legal aid offices and clinics give advice in three main areas. What are they? small claims for wages; disputes between the client and a lender, an installment seller, or a landlord; domestic matters such as divorce, child custody, or the contesting of a will

Examining the Court System

Activity F

Chapter 28

Name_____

Date_____Period_____

Answer the following questions about our court system.

1. What is the purpose of the court system? <u>to try and punish people who have committed criminal</u>
   <u>offenses, to interpret laws, to settle legal problems between people involved in civil disputes</u>

2. What types of cases are tried by state courts? <u>criminal and civil cases involving people within the state</u>

3. What types of cases are tried by federal courts? <u>cases involving federal laws, people from more than one</u>
   <u>state, or cases previously tried at the state level</u>

4. What factors determine the type of court in which a case will be tried? <u>type of case, type of criminal</u>
   <u>offense, value of a civil claim, or whether an original ruling or a review of a previous ruling is being sought</u>

5. Where is a court case first heard? <u>trial court</u>

6. What is a jury? <u>panel of citizens selected to help decide a case in a trial court</u>

7. What happens when a case is appealed? <u>The case goes to a panel of justices in a higher court who review</u>
   <u>the case and either uphold or overturn the trial court's decision.</u>

8. What is the purpose of small claims court? <u>to be more accessible to more people for cases involving small</u>
   <u>amounts of money</u>

9. Tyrone filed a lawsuit against Kate for breach of contract. Who is the plaintiff? <u>Tyrone</u>
   Who is the defendant? <u>Kate</u>